Journey of the Soul

Doris Klein, CSA
Foreword by Robert F. Morneau

SHEED & WARD

Franklin, Wisconsin

As an apostolate of the Priests of the Sacred Heart, a Catholic religious congregation, the mission of Sheed & Ward is to publish books of contemporary impact and enduring merit in Catholic Christian thought and action. The books published, however, reflect the opinions of their authors and are not meant to represent the official position of the Priests of the Sacred Heart.

2000

Sheed & Ward
7373 South Lovers Lane Road
Franklin, Wisconsin 53132
1800-266-5564

Printed in the United States of America

Cover and interior design by Madonna Gauding
Cover art: "Journey of the Soul" by Doris Klein, CSA
Author photo by Mary Luke Baldwin, SSND

Scripture quotations are from the New Revised Standard Version of the Bible, copyright 1946, 1952, and 1971 by the Division of Christian Education of the National Council of the Churches of Christ in the USA. Used by permission. All rights reserved.

Library of Congress Cataloging-in-Publication Data

Klein, Doris, 1949-
    Journey of the soul / Doris Klein ; foreword by Robert F. Morneau.
       p. cm.
    ISBN 1-58051-086-8
       1. Meditations. 2. Spiritual exercises. I. Title.

BV4832.2 .K54 2000+
242--dc21

                                                                                    00-032945
                                                                                    CIP

Acknowledgments

With simple gratitude I acknowledge the many hearts and hands that have brought this book to birth. In particular I thank:

All of the Sisters of St. Agnes, our leadership teams and my local community. Your love and support have invited me to be faithful to my ministry as an artist. All of your names are painted in my heart.

The soul-companions who have journeyed with me. Your mentoring and mirroring have enabled me to bring forth these words and images.

Bob Morneau, not only for graciously writing the Foreword but also for your continued support of my creative work.

The Sheed & Ward staff. I offer my thanks to Tom Hoffman, whose wit and wisdom calmly companioned me through the publication process; to editor, Jeremy Langford and publisher, Stephen Hrycyniak, who believed in and supported this project from the beginning; to Kass Dotterweich, for her sensitive and skilled editing of this manuscript, and to Madonna Gauding, for her creative layout and design.

Contents

Foreword

The journey of the soul, the great adventure we call *spirituality*, is at once highly personal and wonderfully universal. No one duplicates our fingerprints or our soul's generic codes; yet, we all have the same basic capacity to encounter reality, and we all have the same longings for the divine Mystery.

Sister Doris Klein has a deep appreciation for our uniqueness and the universality of the human condition. Her *Journey of the Soul* is an invitational work encouraging readers to trust their own experience of the Sacred in their lives and to take seriously the stirrings of the Spirit—the Spirit of wisdom and beauty that surrounds and sustains us. Using watercolors and words, this gifted artist draws us into her paintings and reflections, not as a stopping point but as a doorway into the presence of God, who works so profoundly in our human experience and in the creative products of artists.

Like the writer Henri J. M. Nouwen, Sister Doris grounds her reflections in the messiness of human life, with all its ambiguities and ambivalences. The adventure is risky and exciting, filled with loss and gain, replete with joys and sorrows. One senses that this artist/author detests sentimentality and soft piety. Life embraces the paschal mystery, that dying and rising process we witness in the gospel, a process that permits little romanticism and demands a tough realism.

Much of spirituality is focused on truth and goodness, and rightly so. Through

Foreword

discernment, we come to know that truth which sets us free; through the practice of virtue that issues forth in goodness, we emulate our God. But there is a third dimension of spirituality—beauty—that needs much more attention. Sister Doris, in her haunting, subtle, nebulous, and provocative watercolors, presents us with drawings that touch the soul in a unique way and elicit a response of wonder and awe that only beauty can do. Our challenge, which she learned from one of her teachers, is not just to look at the paintings but to "walk into them" and see what wonder they hold for us.

Our culture and our religious institutions are in need of alternative images. The old syllogism is still true: "We live on images; images lead to attitudes; attitudes lead to behavior." A work such as *Journey of the Soul* is not a narrative adventure into an artist's heart and soul; rather, it is a work that invites us to encounter a God who will both speak to the heart and send us forth to live fuller lives. The images presented in this volume get us in touch with our deepest self and evoke a response that, through a transformation of attitudes and behavior, impacts society. An authentic spiritual journey always has a social component leading to a sense of solidarity and social justice.

A sampling of the themes in this book gives evidence of an integral spirituality: The Weavers—Walking in Community; Transformation—Moving through Change; Surrender—Letting Go into Love; Integrity—Living in Truth; Roots of Light—Connecting with the Sacred. The dynamic of reaching in and reaching out underlies the truly creative process. Jesus' mission is one of giving life, life to the full (see John 10:10). By grounding our spiritual journey in contemplation and action, we move toward full discipleship.

For me, a central quality in the work of Sr. Doris lies in the adjective "evocative." The marvelous shadings of colors, the primordial circularity of shadowy figures, the expansive movement of energy toward infinity: these are all evocative features that both broaden our experience and help us name our own beauty and longings. This is not catechism with all

Foreword

kinds of answers. Rather, this is a walk into the human experience where the Mystery of God and life wait to embrace us. The "Hound of Heaven," poet Francis Thompson's term for God, is still on the loose in our world.

I've had the privilege of hearing Sr. Doris Klein lecture on her art. In those presentations, she deeply touched her audience as they "walked into" her work, indeed her soul. Many of us experienced transformation and the affirmation that encouraged us to take seriously the inner working of the Spirit of God. The sustained applause we gave her at the lectures I now give her for this present volume. It is a work of discipline and love, of tears and joys, of truth and beauty.

Enter, walk, breathe deeply, be renewed.

Bishop Robert F. Morneau
Auxiliary Bishop of
Green Bay, Wisconsin
April 2000

Introduction

*W*e've all had the experience of seeing something in nature so breathtaking, so magnificent, that it left us speechless. Perhaps it was our first glimpse from a mountaintop or our first taste of the ocean. Maybe we marveled at the bottomless immensity of a canyon or actually descended into the cavernous womb of the earth as we walked into a cave. These types of experiences no doubt left us grasping for words to explain not just what we saw but, more so, *what we knew*. We often find ourselves speechless as we attempt to translate an experience of our soul or catch a glimpse of something that profoundly mirrors the realm of the Divine.

What happens in our deepest being when we hear music that moves us to tears? Somewhere within we experience the wordless language of melody and rhythm that resonates with an essence we *know* in the very cells of our being. What about the painting that stirs us, riveting our eyes on some truth we simply *know* in the core of our heart? What is it in a poem or a dance that distills in few words or movements that *knowing* nod of our experience.

Deep within each of us is an incredible desire to give voice to our profound longing for God. We look with urgency for some language, some words, some images, that will mirror the mystery of the journey of our soul. As we grapple with our efforts to articulate these experiences, we discover that what was perceived to be incredibly complex is, at the same

Introduction

time, profoundly simple. The search for words to describe the experience often leads us to walk with wordlessness.

It is out of this longing and search that these images were born. As I entered the often wordless soul-space of my own spiritual journey, there were times when painting was the only way I could reflect my deeper, intuitive ways of knowing. Once released from my brush, the truth was given a voice outside of myself, and I was better able to translate what I had wordlessly held within. The images began as simple expressions of my journey but, as I began to share them, I realized that they mirrored the soul-experiences we hold in common.

The paintings that follow are done in watercolor which, by its very nature, seems to lend itself to soul-work. The medium is fluid, transparent and, I must confess, sometimes quite messy and hard to control. Yet, all seem apt descriptors for the journey to that deep space within.

Some of these paintings began with a simple wash of color that seemed to mirror for me an insight, feeling, or truth; others seemed to paint themselves. Always, however, even in the abstract images—or perhaps *especially* in the abstract images—these paintings spoke to me of discoveries along the way. In those wordless times, it was the paint that poured out what I needed to hear and say.

These paintings and the accompanying reflections flow from my life and, at the same time, from a much larger place of universal knowing—a knowing that we have in common. For this reason, I have chosen to write the reflections in an inclusive, first-person plural— for this journey is one *we* share. As the artist and author, I simply offer these pages as doorways for each of us to walk through as we explore the themes that flow from our hunger for God. I believe that once a painting leaves my brush it is no longer mine; rather, it belongs to whomever looks at it. And although the words that accompany these

Introduction

paintings are mine, there is considerable blank space meant to invite each of us to our own reflections and explorations of our soul-space. These simple images and words call us to pause and reflect on our own experience and the holy One who walks with us.

Some of these paintings have stories about their creation or inspiration, and I share these stories as the framework and focus for the accompanying reflection. There is, however, no *right* interpretation of a given painting. You may actually discover that the reflection isn't even close to what the image awakens in you personally. Trust that the *real reflection* is the story that arises within as you walk with the color, texture, and words of your own soul-journey, speaking your deepest truth and inner knowing.

As we walk the paths of this journey, we are faced with a longing for and experience of the Divine. It is my intent to continually expand and explore the imagery we use for God. Although I frequently make use of the single word "God" for that Divine, Loving Presence, I implore that we each honor the face of the Sacred that is operative in our respective lives. There is no name big enough for God! None of us is capable of taking in the Mystery in its fullness. As humans, we are compelled to search for the language that translates this experience—yet our words and images fall so short of the unbounded Love.

The language we use for God impacts our reflections on this journey of our soul. God far exceeds the constraint of metaphors that have been heavily layered with patriarchy and judgment. We are continually challenged to take in the understanding of the unconditional love of the Divine for each of us. One of our greatest challenges is to realize, with the apostle Paul, that nothing "in all creation will be able to separate us from the love of God" (Romans 8:39).

On this journey of self-discovery, it will be helpful for us to lean into the teaching of the mystics, who remind us that our longing for God is only a glimmer of God's deep longing for us. We readily assert our profound desire to be one with God and often dedicate much of our life and energy to that end. Are we also willing to believe that it is God who hungers for union with us in infinite and unlimited love? When we ground ourselves in that understanding, we can be seen in our truth, without shame—and know ourselves loved. It is imperative that, as individuals, we reflect on the fact that each of us, female and male, is made in the image and likeness of this loving God. The journey of our soul is simply the journey back to that truth. It is our call to come home to knowing that we are wonderfully made from the moment we were knit together in the womb of God to the present moment where we stand in truth.

The journey you take is uniquely yours, yet the ramifications are like the concentric circles around a stone dropped in a pond. Being attentive to your own voice compels you to act with integrity as you interact in your world. When you lean into the learning of the unconditional Love in which you are created, you cannot help but allow that love to ripple out to others. As you walk with compassion for yourself, you free a compassion that reaches well beyond the parameter of your experience into the larger community, and to a fullness and abundance that can only be the Sacred Soul of Love.

I am always taken by the wonderfully diverse ways in which people "walk" through books. Some of us, for example, are cover-and-spine people: if the book has a beautiful cover, a title that cuts to the chase, and pictures, well, it has already served its purpose! Some of us, however, start at the beginning of a book and sequentially turn each page until we reach the end. Then there are those table-of-contents surveyors, those who selectively choose chapters that seem pertinent and then go directly to that material. And finally, there are those who simply open the book anywhere—and go from there in trust. This book is intended to be used in any and all of these ways.

As this work came together, I struggled with the sequence, wondering if there was a "logical" or progressive order in which the pieces should appear. This process itself was a

Introduction

realization that the spiritual path is no straight line but a uniquely winding road, challenging each of us to find our own "sequence" and "order" to things. Thus, this book is designed to be sipped slowly, inviting us to sit with and savor the stories of our soul. The reflections are intentionally brief and are shared only to spark a personal response to the image or story. When we walk into the paintings or sit with the reflections, we may well recognize themes, feelings, or images not directly noted or even evident. Remember that those insights are critical pieces of our own personal soul-story and need to be reverenced and honored. After all, there are as many descriptions and reflections as there are individuals who open this book. We have to trust our own individual responses!

Each reflection closes with a section titled "Suggested Reflection Process," a tool that offers ways in which you might explore the themes of your own soul-journey. It is my hope that the paintings, reflections, and suggestions will be doorways into your inner wisdom. I had a wonderful art professor who implored, "Don't just *look* at a painting! *Go for a walk inside* and see where it leads you." That is my suggestion as well; each of us is invited to walk inside this book and find the places where it leads us on the unique journey of our soul.

Notes on "Suggested Reflection Process"

The "Suggested Reflection Process" that follows each painting and reflection is to be used as a tool in exploring further the presented theme or focus. Sometimes all we need is an invitation to unfold the wonderful, creative gifts given to assist us as we explore the mysteries of God and our spiritual journey. We often shy away from this process, however, minimizing our creative energy. We must be careful not to confuse *creative expression* with *performance* or *technical skill*. The use of painting, writing, movement, and music will often bypass our more linear, evaluative patterns, and allow us to access wonderful insights we have hidden deep within. We simply have to bear in mind that the *process* not the *product* is the critical component that leads us to some of the unspoken truths for which we often have no voice. If we can put aside our judgments and shame as we engage in these activities, and experiment with where they lead us, we may be happily surprised at the secrets of our soul! In this work, I include a diversity of options and forms of expression that might lead to the wisdom and insight of intuition and creativity.

Creative Writing

Because writing is such a common form of expression for the human being, it helps to have some focused methods by which you can access your more intuitive inner places. When you become lost in the density of your emotions and inner judgments, writing can serve as a tool to help you clarify what is going on. The process of writing puts a framework of words around the experience, allowing you to name what's happening. Once written, however, your words must take on their natural audible essence; thus it can be helpful if you read aloud what you've written. You may, at times, choose to share your reflections with someone else, but you first must be aware of the distinct value of hearing your *own* voice speaking your *own* words to your *own* soul. Reading your own words aloud in a safe place allows you to be attentive to what you hear and feel without judgment or inhibitions.

Those of us who have a difficult time focusing may find it helpful to write with our nondominant hand, the one we normally do not use. This will slow down our racing or confused mind and allow us to touch into the information we hold in the less frequently accessed side of our brain.

The following formats are suggested *ways* of writing:

THE MANTRA: A mantra is a simple, short, inspirational line expressing a personal or universal truth; the power of a mantra is directness, brevity, and repetition. A few mantras are given in this book but some of the most powerful ones are those you write for yourself. The key to a mantra's effectiveness is to repeat it over the course of days and weeks, until it becomes part of you. Saying a mantra out loud helps you in the learning process. You also may want to place the written mantra where you can read it often as a reminder to hold that piece of truth.

THE TOPICAL POEM: Poetry is an invitation to distill a theme or experience into a kernel of truth. The topical poem, or any other poetry format with which you might be familiar, can help you focus on a topic. The topical poem follows a specific format:

Notes on "Suggested Reflection Process"

First line: a noun

Second line: two adjectives

Third line: three verbs

Fourth line: a four-word phrase

Fifth line: a noun that repeats the idea of the first line in a new way

Once you have reflected for several minutes on a specific theme or image, you can translate that truth further in a topical poem. Once the poem is finished, take your truth even further by reading the piece slowly and out loud two or three times. If you enjoy this form of expression, you might want to keep the series of poems together in a notebook or journal, reading them at a later date in the sequence they were originally written.

TIMED WRITING: This exercise is designed to help you bypass those many inner censors and judgments that might keep you from speaking your truth. Begin by choosing a place where you can write without interruption, and a topic or word that you want to reflect on. After a short period of reflection, set a timer so that you don't have to pay attention to the clock—and begin writing. Write whatever comes to mind, without stopping, ignoring grammar and spelling concerns. Your expressions are to include feelings and images that arise in the process. If you don't know what to write, write: "I don't know what to write." During your allotted time, do not stop and re-read what you've written—just keep writing. When the time is up, stop and immediately read, *out loud*, what you've written. You may want to follow this first session with a second period of writing on a single word or issue that surfaced in your original writing. Simply remember that the process is meant to loosen the words and images that you may tend to screen out. Sometimes critical information is missed if you skip reading your writing out loud.

Notes on "Suggested Reflection Process"

Visual Arts

The well-worn line, "A picture paints a thousand words," isn't just about other people's art! The process of using art media may surprise us with profound insights, especially since much "soul-stuff" is nonverbal. When using painting and drawing to explore the themes of our journey, we may need to consciously set aside any judgments or shame we experience with regard to our skills. Too many of us carry old messages that left us feeling shamed and embarrassed about our artistic abilities. We simply must remember that this is not about producing art but entering soul-space.

One way to bypass this inner critic is to use your nondominant hand for written or drawn expressions. Not only can this be a "good excuse" when you begin to criticize your own work, but, more importantly, it can open the information you hold in the less frequently accessed side of your brain. Another option is to draw with your eyes closed. Again, the process closes down the judgments, and the very movement of your arms and hands can open an intuitive insight. The idea is to play and have fun—not analyze! You want to let the feel of the media and the movement lead you wherever it goes. You might want to try using different substances, like nonhardening clay, finger paints—and don't forget good old crayons! Crayons, after all, hold secrets of the past as well as the unfolding of the future.

Once you're finished with your visual expression, take the time to sit with your work or keep it in a place where it will visually remind you of what you explored. You may choose to share your work with others who companion you in soul-space—but exercise caution. You want to select individuals and places that are safe, since visual art often touches very sacred and intimate insights that need to be reverenced and honored. If your work is extremely sensitive, you must choose adequately prepared professionals to companion you in this process.

Notes on "Suggested Reflection Process"

Music

You may choose to use music in a variety of ways. As in the writing processes, it is important to hear your own voice. What's more, the same is true about musical expressions as with other artistic expressions: you may carry old messages about your abilities. As long as you remember that singing, toning, or playing an instrument is not about giving a recital but, rather, about giving voice to your soul-song, you will be able to relax into the process.

Something as simple as centering while you tone a single note or repeat a phrase can quiet your inner spaces and connect you to the earth. At times, you may want to select a specific piece of recorded music that seems to resonate with your reflection. If you find such a piece, you will want to play it a number of times so that it begins to become *your* music, singing along—out loud—until you know what it really holds for you. Writing your own music—melody, words, or both—can be helpful. Sometimes composing a one-line melody to resonate with a mantra you have written can become a touchstone that brings you back when you wander from your truth. Drumming, too, can open deep pockets of insight and voice the full range of human emotions.

Because we often allow music to be just another level of background noise in our busyness, we have to listen carefully to the melodies and instruments that mirror our soul-space. This requires a quiet surrounding where we can be at one with the piece, allowing the music to pour into our cells and out of our body as we hear it with our heart and sing it with our soul.

Notes on "Suggested Reflection Process"

Movement

So often we associate spirituality and soul-work with sitting quietly and attentively, taking it in from the outside. We act as if we are passive observers in the process instead of standing and moving in truth. Dance is a way for us to give voice to our entire body as it translates the workings of our inner spirit, allowing us to engage in the activity of soul-work. Too often we pass judgment on our bodies and thus minimize this rich voice of insight. How better to loosen feelings that are stuck within than to move and run and shake and dance! Let it go!

You may want to experiment with this, choosing simple body postures or movement to give expression to feelings of joy, anger, fear, or despair. You might ask yourself, "What does it feel like in my body when I reflect on . . . (one of the themes of this book)?" Remembering to honor your physical ways of knowing, you can consciously dance, walk, and use your arms, hands, and legs to translate what you feel inside. You may want to find a safe and, if necessary, solitary setting where you can comfortably express what you know in the depths of your soul through the voice of your body.

Guided Imagery

We all have had experiences of "picturing" in our mind a place, an event, a sound, or a color. "Imaging things" can also help us calm our spirit amid the busyness of our lives, especially when we use inner imagery to take us to a given setting. Although there are many written and recorded guided imageries available that may be helpful, they often, for various reasons, fall short of our needs.

Notes on "Suggested Reflection Process"

As you reflect on the given paintings and images offered in this book, I recommend writing or recording any images that come to mind. After all, who better to guide you as you walk this spiritual path than the companion of your own self! It is amazingly insightful to hear your own voice inviting you to breathe, to walk into an image, and to meet the truth of your heart. You know your own timing, the places that bring you to quiet, and the images of the Holy One who walks with you there in those places.

These are only a few suggestions that might be helpful as we reflect on the journey of our soul. Many of us have our own tried-and-true ways that assist us in our spiritual reflection process. For those who would like to explore further, there are many good books that offer specific details on ways to give voice to our soul. Regardless of the means we choose, however, we want to honor the ways that are best for us. As we explore the images and reflections that follow, we want to trust the wisdom of our wonderful, creative, intuitive self, as we plumb the mysteries of God and our spiritual journey.

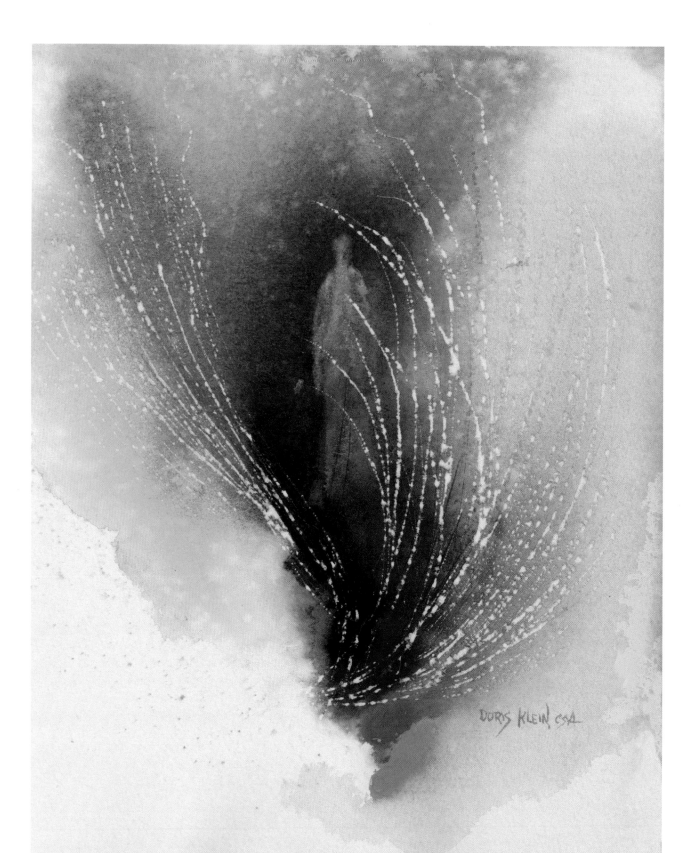

DORIS KLEIN CSA

1. Journey of the Soul

Walking Our Sacred Path

*W*e are each given the gift of our journey. Some days we walk with delight and a lightness that is filled with clarity and focus, confidently proceeding with the knowledge that we are companioned and supported as our life unfolds. Walking with a sense of purpose, we embrace the challenges that lure us ahead. We enjoy the company of those who walk beside us, and we are energized by their support.

During these times of clarity and focus, our awareness of the Divine Presence is amazingly vivid, and our faith, commitment, and dedication to serving others seem to sustain us with energy and strength. The map seems clear, the obstacles seem manageable, and our provisions seem substantial. We walk with the assurance of knowing that there is nothing that can keep us from Love!

Then gradually, or sometimes suddenly, the terrain changes. The light dims and the clarity fades. The path appears muddy, and the options seem to be multiple and confusing. Our confidence wanes as we wonder if we have enough to sustain us. We notice that the companions around us seem to have disappeared, and we feel incredibly alone. While our energies and desires drain, the obstacles that confront us grow to appear insurmountable, and we wonder where God is—the One we were once so sure walked with us. Sometimes it feels like a desert; at other times, it feels like a steep descent into hollow emptiness. Seemingly alone, often exhausted, we wonder why we have been led into this wilderness and if we will ever emerge from it. We begin to question if this journey really is gift.

Journey of the Soul

The landscape here cannot be neatly compartmentalized into simple dualistic images of clarity or confusion. We are each familiar with the struggle of maintaining our pace through the "partly cloudy" days, wondering what happened to the spring in our step. The status quo grows monotonous, and our inspiration dims as we wander in a flat landscape of faded color. Our robot-like completion of tasks leaves us without a sense of purpose, and even God seems to be absorbed into the grayness around us.

We all know these various terrains along our journey. We recognize the times of clarity, when we have been filled with inspiration, dedication, and love, and we tend to call these the "good times," the "gifted times," the times we cling to and so desire to hold forever. Yet, the other passages are, indeed, gift as well. We may not want to believe that, yet these more arid places are often the points of our journey where we come to know that we do not make this sojourn alone. Here we learn that this is not some cross-country walk for which we have physically prepared ourselves. Rather, this is a soul-journey, one that requires we focus all the gifts of our body, mind, and spirit as we move through this way of being and knowing into the Landscape of Love. The journey demands we continue to lighten our load, as we let go of those attitudes, illusions, relationships, and things that prevent us from being at one with God. In this trek we come face to face with our shadows, our fears, our gifts, and our goodness. As we pass through the many changes, we continue to learn to walk with integrity, compassion, wisdom, and abundance. Indeed, there are times when we stall, resist, even resent the challenges, and, faced with doubt and despair, sure we have been abandoned in this God-forsaken warp.

Yet, somehow, we are led by God's grace to breathe, to trust, to move into a deeper Knowing. Layer by layer, our illusions fall aside as we come to know more clearly that we have been and always are loved. Once more, what we have learned in the light is carried with us into the dark and, little by little, the geography feels less confusing as we journey closer home to our truth.

This soul-journey is the process of spiraling into the Heart of the Holy where, in reality, we always are. We simply learn to see more clearly.

Suggested Reflection Process ⟩

Using the metaphors and images of landscape, reflect on the terrain of your soul-journey. It may be helpful to choose a specific time or event to focus your reflection in an imagery that uses tangible metaphors such as a meadow, desert, forest, etc. Set the scene by describing the sensory elements of what you see, hear, smell, and feel. As you walk in this space, image your divine Companion with you and be attentive to the message the Holy One offers. When you have finished, you may want to record your experience by drawing or writing about it.

2. Dragonfly

Facing Our Illusions

$\mathcal{T}$he indigenous people of the North American tribes have the rich tradition of totem animals that offer accompaniment and assistance on the journey of life. It is their belief that these animal companions bring a specific medicine or lesson as we walk our path. The dragonfly, for example, is said to bring the medicine needed to break through illusions that have kept us from standing in the truth, beauty, and poise of who we were created to be.

As I explored the image of the dragonfly and the task of breaking through those illusions in my own life, I began a painting. I composed this piece on a full sheet of watercolor paper and experienced a great feeling of expansiveness as I drew the top form. I wanted the dragonfly reflected in the water, because I sensed a need to ponder and reflect on the illusions that have been part of my life.

At one point, however, I stopped working on this piece and allowed it simply to sit in my studio for nearly six months. I was *afraid* to go any further. After all, I might ruin it; I might mess it up; I might not be able to do it right. And thus unfolded another learning of the dragonfly, as I peeled off yet one more layer of my illusions.

Then one day, I decided to just begin. I put the pigment on the wings in various spots and sprayed the piece with water. The color ran free and brilliant, and the energy was released, leaving the wings expansive and full of light.

Dragonfly

As each of us is called to face the illusions in our life, we must continue to touch into the most basic belief that we are wonderfully made in the image and likeness of God. We are created in love, and we are beautiful. Although this is, indeed, a simple statement, we often spend the better part of our lives attempting to claim that truth, because it has become so layered with lies and illusions. The experiences and teachings of our childhood, the patterns and pressures of our society, even the messages and modeling of our institutional religions, have clouded the basic truth that we are wonderfully made.

The dark waters in the lower portion of the work are reflective of the soul-space we must ponder as we attempt to name and let go of all that prevents us from flying free in truth, grace, poise, and beauty. Nestled in those dark waters, we often find our patterns of shame as we face the fears of not being enough and not having enough. Here we are asked to grapple with the lies that have prevented us from standing in truth. To reflect in this soul-space demands that we ask the hard questions and listen in honesty as we dare to answer from the place of our deepest knowing.

What are the roots of our fear? Could it be that pervasive sense that if others *really* knew us they would go away? Can we dare to be seen as we are and trust that we will still be loved? Perhaps we struggle with the lies that support our envy of others. After all, if we only had what that person has, then we would be okay. How certain we are that others have more and we don't have enough. And of course, since we dare not let anyone else know our fear of being less than enough, we find ways to convince them that we are, in fact, more. We assess what we believe they want or find desirable, and attempt to measure up. In the process, however, we often abandon ourselves and our own truth.

Some of the illusions are manifested in our false sense of control and are deeply rooted in the belief that there is only one right way. And because we believe we know the right way, we certainly expect and often demand that others ascribe to that way as well.

Conversely, we sometimes are sure that everyone else knows the right way and ours is certainly wrong. Control issues also spring from these fears and lies: if there is chaos or lack of control, we surely will fall apart. At some levels we believe that if there is conflict, we will die; thus we strive for peace at any price, even if the price is our integrity. The list goes on and on.

No one else can identify those illusions that prevent us from being faithful to who we are; that is something we must do ourselves. The critical move in facing our illusions is to ask for the courage to name, without judgment, those attitudes and patterns that are false covers. It is a time to ask for divine intercession and compassion to guide us into these obsidian soul-spaces as we identify the lies and false hopes that we have carried for so long. To name our fears will not destroy us; rather, such honest naming will enable us to dissipate the anxiety that accompanies them. We must breathe here and cling to the undergirding truth that we were created in love to be who we were made to be. Dare we believe that and hold it as firmly as we have held onto the illusions?

As we face these illusions, there are times when we must seek companionship and witnesses. When the lies are deeply rooted and too frightening to face alone, skilled professionals such as spiritual directors, therapists, or trained counselors can assist us. Of course, the very act of asking for companionship sometimes brings us face to face with yet another illusion, that we can do it by ourselves!

In this process of breaking through our illusions, we must recognize that it is simply that, a process. Each layer invites us to pause, breathe, and remember that we are companioned by a loving God who sees us in our truth and loves us. Freed of the lies and false hopes, we recognize the grace and truth in which we were made, and are able to fly more freely with poise.

Suggested Reflection Process ⟩⟩

As you sit with the image of the dragonfly, do a timed writing exercise using one of the following suggestions:

✳ Think about a word or feeling that surfaced as you looked at the painting or read the reflection, and write whatever comes to mind.

✳ Complete one of the following phrases:

> "My great fear is that . . . "
>
> "If only I had . . . , then I . . . "
>
> "I really don't like admitting that . . . "

After completing your writing, be sure to read it out loud and do a second session on a word, phrase, or feeling that surfaced.

3. Walk into Mystery

Entering the Darkness

*T*his painting is a reflection on our journey into the darkness, a place of few words and images. It began as a muddy, gray piece that seemed hopeless, destined only to be pitched. As a last ditch effort to save the paper, I squeezed a horizon line of red-violet pigment across the sheet and flooded the page with water. And there, in the run of the wash, I recognized a solitary figure lost in the magenta mist. Attempting to define the image, I dabbed around her, discovering a companion figure that had been there all along.

When we face those times of uncertainty in our life, the scene is often blurry. Things we were so sure of suddenly make little sense. The answers we thought were clear now seem lost in a distant fog, and we wander aimlessly, unable to regain the focus we once believed we had. Our confusion is unsettling. Doubt, like vertigo, distorts our balance as we fearfully wander in a vast and empty inner wilderness. As we wrestle with the darkness, a rush of panic washes into our hearts, our breath becomes shallow and, with each question, the judgments seem to escalate. Surely there must be a way out of here!

This experience is different for each of us. Sometimes this soul-space is met in times of discernment, as we try to unearth the choice that is "right." During these times, we grapple with options, hoping that amid the chaos we will find clarity. We listen for the voice of our heart, our truth, but seem only to hear the deafening throb of our uncertainty. At other times, this space wears the colors of our deepest self-doubt. We bury ourselves beneath the fears that we won't have what we need and, in the process, we lose sight of our integrity and worth. The old patterns of fretting make us dizzy, and we fall into despair. Perhaps this place is marked by times of nothing—no thoughts, no feelings, no insights, no inspirations—and a bland mediocrity of the soul seems to stretch forever.

Dare we believe that in this walk of mystery we are companioned even when we feel so desperately alone? Is it possible that the voice of God is in the voice of the silence and the darkness? This painting is an invitation for us to breathe in this place where we so often hold our breath. It reminds us to lean into the sometimes hidden Presence that befriends us in this empty and alone time. We, like the figure in the foreground, often walk unaware of the ever present, ever loving Companion.

When these times of mystery seem endless and our souls become weary of the stretch to believe, our prayer must be a simple request—that we be reminded that we have not been abandoned in this place to wander forever alone. The fleck of orange paint that was accidentally lodged in the heart of the figure in the foreground is perhaps that very reminder, for it is often a silent flicker in our heart, the tiny voice within, that whispers wordlessly, "You are always loved. You are never alone."

Suggested Reflection Process ⤳

Use timed writing, the topical poem format, or any expressive media of your choice to explore one of the following question:

 ✳ How do I name this wilderness place in my soul journey?

 ✳ What are my experiences of walking in the dark mystery?

When you finish, sit with the image and simply breathe for a few minutes, as you honor the emotions and stories that arise.

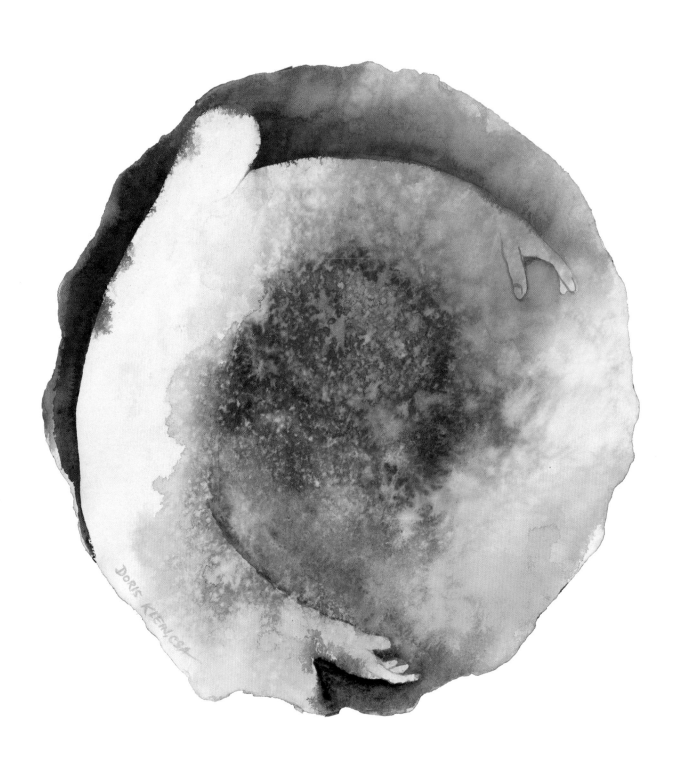

4. Abundance

Opening to Fullness

I painted this piece when I was at a critical juncture in my life, a time of passage into a new way of being. Although I felt determined and prepared to move on, I was terrified of letting go. I needed an expression of gratitude for the gifts I had received along that part of my journey, and a reflection of the spacious Heart that would hold me as I grieved all I was leaving behind. I wanted a visual reminder that I had more than enough and was held in infinite Abundance, even when I felt empty and alone.

Our patterns often find us looking at life from a perspective of deprivation—and this is not surprising. Society saturates us with messages that we don't have enough, that we are incomplete, that we need more. This view blinds us to the abundance that is ours, and necessitates a conscious effort to open our hearts to the fullness that is already there. It is this "great-fullness" in each of us that mirrors our abundant God.

When our world closes in on us, we become mired in petty ways of interacting. Stuck in the fear that we don't have enough, we grasp even more tightly to what we think we need. There, in our perceived neediness, we hope that a material possession, a certain relationship, or special position of power might somehow complete us—and *then* we will have enough, we will be complete, we will need for nothing more. Sadly, this grasping tends to shrink our trust and heightens our illusions of control, leaving us weary and spent, our energy wasted. What we cling to often dissolves in our grasp, and we reach, once again, for more at any cost.

Abundance

By contrast, gratitude is expansive, leading us outward beyond ourselves. It connects us with the larger presence of fullness reflected in our earth, our universe, our cosmos—all of which mirrors the immensity of the Spirit. As we consciously develop and practice the discipline of gratitude, we are challenged to look with eyes that recognize a Greatness too extensive to hold.

The rhythm of gratitude is beautifully modeled in a Jewish prayer, called "Dayenu," used at Passover:

How many are the wonderful things that have

happened to us for which we give thanks to God!

Had He (God) simply delivered us from Egypt

and not set us on our way, Dayenu!

  (That would be enough!)

Had He (God) set us on our way,

  crossing with us the barrier of the sea,

and not led us through the wastelands, Dayenu!

  (That would be enough!)

Had He (God) cared for us

  during our wanders through the wastelands

and not ordained us for the Sabbath, Dayenu!

  (That would be enough!)

Abundance

Had He (God) ordained us on the Sabbath

and not brought us to Sinai, Dayenu!

   (That would be enough!)[1]

The prayer goes on with more verses recounting the blessings of the people in their passage. The rhythm of this song can lead us to our own "Dayenu!" as we voice our gratitude in a litany of recognition of the multiple layers of gifts we have been given. Our greed and grasping would fall away if only we could more readily recognize the abundance that surrounds us.

To stand in this attitude requires an intentional practice, a discipline of mindfulness, a full awareness of the abundance with which we walk. There are those times, of course, when we are so aware of the multiple gifts and blessings that surround us that we simply radiate gratitude. At other times, however, especially when we experience pain, confusion, and loss, our attitude of abundance becomes critical. I think of a wonderful soul-sister of mine who, when I am in the midst of an insight, even the more painful ones, will look directly into my eyes and say, "Now you be sure to thank!" It is this practice and rhythm of gratitude that will surface and remind us that we continue to have what we need—even when we fear we may not.

It is with a great-full heart that we can move through some of our most difficult passages and simply *thank*, not for the pain but for the compassionate Presence that companions us there. We are able to lean into God, even though we may not always feel it, and hold to the deep knowing that we will continue to have what we need. Walking in trust, we embrace what is given, recognizing that, indeed, we do have enough. This perspective— that of a full heart— enables us to tap an energy we never believed possible, leaving us with a freedom of movement that allows us to mirror to others the abundance that is of God.

Suggested Reflection Process ༀ

Enter into one of the following experiences:

✳   Write and/or speak out loud the "Dayenu!" of your soul-journey, ending each phrase with, " . . . and that would be enough!"

✳   Identify an image that reflects how you feel when you face your fear of not having enough. It might be helpful to draw, paint, or sculpt that image.

✳   Lie on the floor or outside on the ground if possible, and feel the earth supporting you. With each breath, feel each part of your body touching the surface beneath you as you let go of your need to support yourself. Once quieted, direct your attention to an experience of natural beauty, such as a mountain, a cave, a forest, or a blade of grass, and enter that image. If, for example, you pictured the ocean, see yourself on the shore, feel the expansive sky overhead, the warm sun on your face, the breeze tossing your hair, the sand under your feet. See the stretching beach, and hear the endless rhythm of the waves. Let your energy connect with the expansiveness of God, and be at one with of the Creator who holds you in Love.

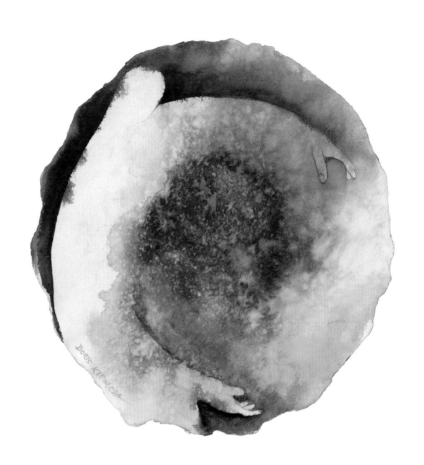

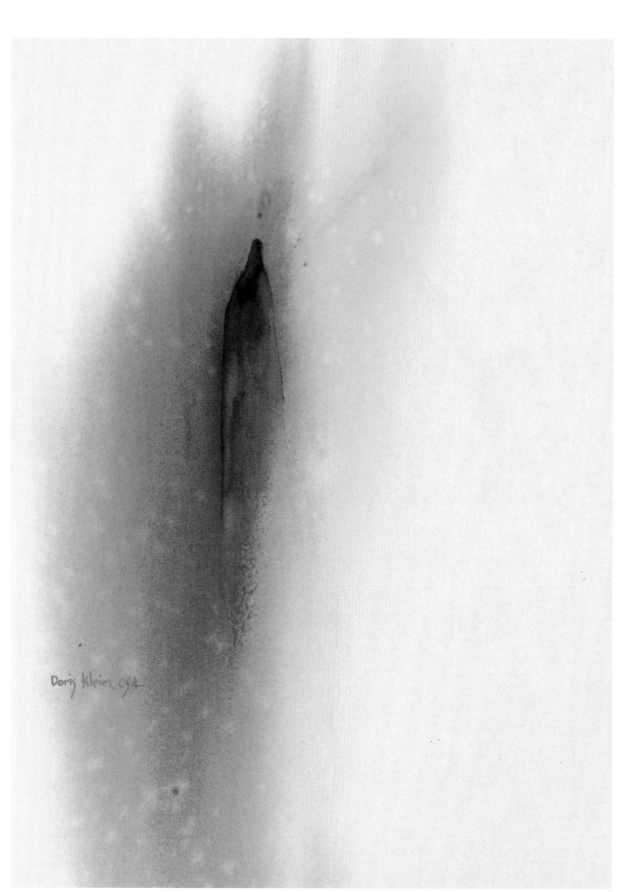

5. Discernment

Standing in Decision

*A*t one time or another, we have all stood in that awkward, messy in-between place where, faced with decisions and choices, we long for clarity. In that place, we attempt to find answers by putting situations in opposing positions, as if we could simply say, "This is the right way and that is the wrong way." Rather, we are challenged to be faithful to the process of holding the larger truths while listening to the voice of integrity within.

Too often, we slip into the dualistic belief that there is a distinct either/or way of splitting complex choices into two opposing ideas. The comparative stance finds us believing that one excludes the other, assuming an "all or nothing" attitude that traps within it the information we really need for discernment. We construct air-tight compartments into which we neatly try to isolate all the pieces of information, hoping that the structure will clarify the decision.

When trying to make difficult choices, we often begin by gathering factual information and making lists to substantiate the advantage of one alternative over the others. In addition, we seek input from the "authorities" around us, certain that trusted and respected others will tell us what to do or at least affirm our choice. So often in the process, we fail, or perhaps *fear*, to trust the wisdom of our own intuition.

Discernment is an invitation to be attentive to the voices of our deep inner knowing. It demands time to quiet the outer noises and listen to our heart and our body which, when

Discernment

we walk in integrity, will tell the truth, even a truth we may not want to hear. To listen within, we must breathe into the sacred connection we have with the holy One, asking to be still and attentive. The process demands a discipline as we repeatedly quiet the thoughts, judgments, and fears that bubble so quickly in our minds. Gently but firmly, as if guiding a young child, we must hush the hounding of our head and descend into the cave of our heart.

This place of knowing speaks a language that is often wordless. As we sit with our options, we will find that images and feelings unfold, bringing us vital information. "What do I feel in my body when I hold each choice? What are the emotions that wash through me? If I could really do what I wanted, what would that be like? What image comes to my mind as I picture myself in the various options?" As we ask our own questions, whatever they may be, we slowly pull aside the debris that traps our energy and insight here in this in-between place.

At times, the blending of the intuitive and the linear information bursts forth with a clarity that almost tips us over—and at that moment, we just *know*! It's a simple, clear choice that resonates with integrity through our entire being. And, although we may have difficulty verbalizing or translating the clarity to others, we know in our heart what we must do, and we begin.

At other times, however, we become paralyzed by fear and feel cemented in this awkward in-between place for what seems like an eternity. We feel overwhelmed with what we can't seem to figure out. Our first challenge in these stuck moments is to breathe. Even though the chaos and confusion are deafening, Wisdom walks with us here as we simply wait to know. Perhaps this decision has a longer gestation time than we would like, and perhaps the process will invite us to walk new paths we have never before considered. Sometimes, however, the decision is *not* to decide, and we continue walking, carrying our options.

Discernment

Sadly, our linear minds often deem the shortest and most direct route as the best, yet it serves us well to recount the insights and gifts gained in the round-about way we may have to take. For example, there may be times when we recognize the need to reconsider, to retrace our steps, to revisit the questions, so that we can learn even more about ourselves and our options. Rather than fall into the trap of judging our decision harshly, perhaps we need to give thanks for what we have discovered in a process that winds and overlaps upon itself.

In the end, we may uncover choices or answers that we'd rather deny, running from what we know is true. Perhaps we had hoped for a different solution, something easier, something more pleasant, something less disruptive of our life or the lives of those around us. Acting with integrity demands courage as we ask to be faithful to the truth we have mined in this deep discovery, praying to act wisely and walk mindfully along this ever unfolding path.

Finally, we must not limit the term discernment to those major life choices, forgetting the daily decisions that invite and challenge us to be attentive to the voice within. Mindful of the multiple times we strive to hear the call of the Holy, we ask simply to be attentive to the many ways God speaks, as we slowly and patiently listen with our whole being for the whispers that lead us.

Suggested Reflection Process ✕

As you reflect on a specific time of discernment, or a choice or decision you are presently processing, picture yourself as the figure in this painting. What are the colors around you? Describe what is clear and what is blurry in your process. Name what you feel in your body as you walk with the choices before you. Simply sit for a few minutes with your eyes closed, your hands open, your palms up resting in your lap, and feel yourself gently holding all the options and insights you are given.

You might find it helpful to walk or run with your discernment. Carry a question with you as you move along, mindfully returning to it when your thoughts stray. To support your discernment when you find yourself becoming distracted or running from the question, carry with you a short mantra such as "Breathe!" or "I have what I need." Repeat it to bring you back to your focus.

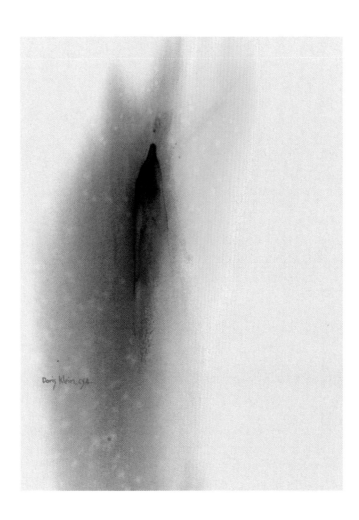

Rooted in Wisdom—
Connecting at the
Heart

New Ventures
'99

DORIS KLEIN, CSA

6. Rooted in Wisdom

Connecting at the Heart

When I was asked to participate as an "artist articulator" at a conference, I was directed specifically to translate the spirit and movement of the assembly into a painting. The gathering, "New Ventures," focused on entrepreneurial ministries and brought together women from religious communities across the country who were seeking support and insight from the wisdom and experience of the assembly. As I sat with them for three days, I recognized that, although critical information was made available, it was the inner wisdom rooted deeply within each participant that gave heart to the ministries in which these women were engaged. My attempt to paint this experience led me to the image of a tree as the metaphor for each of us as we seek the gift of wisdom.

Wisdom, frequently linked with linear information, is often perceived to be outside of ourselves. We consider reading one more book, taking one more course, seeking the advice of one more authority, hoping somehow to answer the questions and challenges of our life journey. We tend to think that the information we collect in our head, the "top of our tree," is wisdom. We recognize and respect this linear component and draw much from those whose scope of experience and insight appears to be well beyond ours. Yet, the information we gather is only one of the elements of wisdom. The input of others must be brought within, "down into our roots," where we are challenged to blend it with our own deep knowing.

Rooted in Wisdom

Too often, we readily assign the gift of wisdom to another—at the cost of denying our own. In a dualistic, comparative model, we see wisdom measured on a hierarchical thermometer, and ascribe to ourselves a below-normal temperature. "After all," we think, "she can do this so much better" or "He knows so much more." We place these people on pedestals, certain that if they were in our shoes, they certainly would know what to do. By envying what others have, we minimize what we really know and give away our own authority and power.

There are those times, too, when we mask our fear of not knowing by presumptuously assuming a stance of power over others, using our knowledge to intimidate with a condescending air of authority. True wisdom, however, simply and humbly acknowledges that we know what we know, each of us, and that we each bring a piece of the truth—no more, no less. Mentors and models of true wisdom bring the experience of their lives tempered with humility and integrity and, as they walk beside us, enable us to uncover our own wisdom.

Intuitive knowing—the insight, the inspiration, the "I just know"—we hear deep within is a vital voice of wisdom that we sometimes hesitate to trust. Yet, if we are to sort through, examine, and explore our own deeply rooted insights, we must enter a quieter, more reflective stance. To be attentive to the voice of wisdom within, we must enter the quiet cave of our heart and sit in the seat of our own truth.

We were each created in the image and likeness of God, and we mirror the face of God in the uniqueness of who we are. It is not a comparative more than/less than model, but a collaborative sharing of the unbounded wisdom of Sophia. The Old Testament Book of Wisdom ascribes a feminine personification to wisdom and, later in history, wisdom is attributed the name Sophia, who awaits within the deep intuitive cave of our heart. Here we gather all of the information—experiential, linear, and intuitive—and hold it in the light of Sophia, the "wisdom face of God." When we connect to her in the depths of our heart, we stand firmly rooted in our own truth, insight, and wisdom.

Suggested Reflection Process ✕

Draw a line midway across a piece of paper. Above the line, draw a simple tree trunk with branches reaching outward and upward. As you draw the branches, bring to mind the sources you look to for information, and write these on the branches of the tree. These sources may be people, programs, events, or experiences that provide you with input when you face choices or need guidance in daily life.

Below the line, begin to draw a root system and explore the ways that you recognize and honor your own intuitive wisdom. Identify your reflective patterns and processes of discernment and decision making that come from your heart.

When you complete your tree, the branches overhead and the root system below, reflect on the balance between the branches and the roots, not simply by size or number but by the value and importance you place on each component.

Write a topical poem that reflects on your own wisdom.

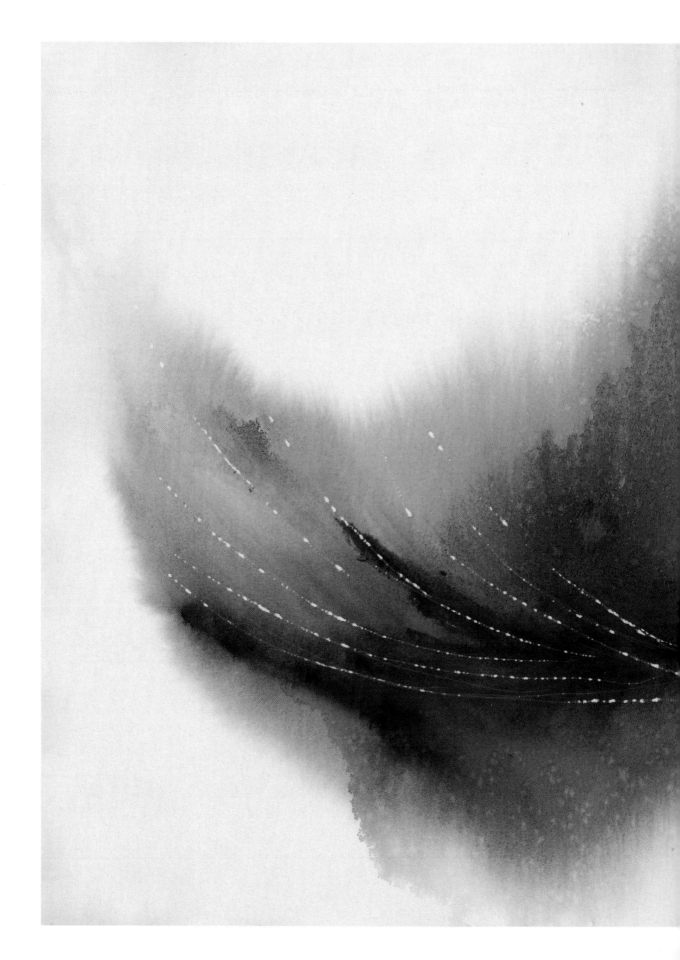

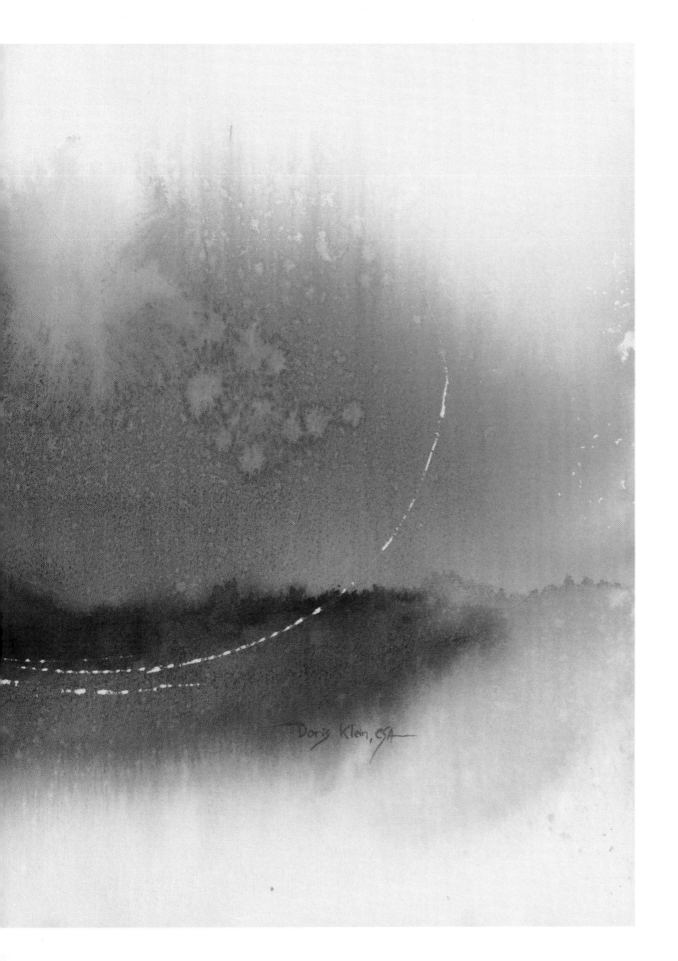

Doris Klein, CSA

7. The Sea in Me

Exploring the Waters of the Soul

There are times when no words or images can adequately describe those fluid places within where we are at one with our deepest knowing; places where we connect to the Divine Womb of Wisdom; places where, even in the darkness, we are held in love. Yet, the rich imagery of water does touch our deepest and earliest memory of being, reminding us of our wordless beginnings of life. This fluid metaphor reflects the expansiveness of our intuitive way of knowing that we often hesitate to trust.

The image of a panicky swimmer also comes to mind, mirroring our struggle to stay in the linear, verbal space of our head rather than dive into the lower realms of deep feeling and intuitive knowing. Because society has programmed us to trust our head not our heart, we use dualistic judgments about intuitive insight and label it as unreliable and "unquantifiable" when compared to linear, rational thought. When we support the minimization of intuition, however, we deny ourselves the benefit of some of our deepest wisdom. We resist relaxing into this space, allowing our fear to keep us from the richness of balance. The vastness of these waters can be overwhelming, but to enter them is to sink more fully into the ocean of divine Love who offers us the expansive insight of our heart.

Many secrets are held in the depths of our soul, often trapped under years of hiding. Sometimes there are many layers of shame and guilt that must be washed away before we are able to reach the core of our truth. At times, however, the fury of our emotions can deter us from exploring and giving voice to our inner truth. For example, hearing the old message that feelings can't be trusted and should be hidden from view, we too often let the fluidity of our tears frightens us. We were taught, after all, not to "fall apart," to "keep it together." Some of us have suffered so long with this old message that we are afraid, ashamed, or perhaps even unable to answer the question, "What do I really feel?" Yet, not to be attentive to these voices is to deprive ourselves of some of the most truthful insights held in these deep soul-waters.

Our soul, where we are most deeply connected with God, is often a wordless place of simply knowing what we know. It holds waves of insight, feeling, and wisdom, beckoning us to dive into the mystery of the intuitive. We often enter these waters through the mirrors given us by the poets, musician, artists, and mystics who swim with us here. Their modeling and mentoring enable us to trust ourselves as we give voice to the artist, musician, poet, and mystic within ourselves. How many times have we seen or heard something that resonated with that place of knowing, causing us to weep or giving us goose bumps? Were we not connecting at some level with the Sacred? With practice we become more confident in our own wisdom as we continue to discover the treasure we hold here.

The Beloved invites us to enter these soul-waters and surrender to the unconditional Love that supports and sustains us. There, the voices of our deep, intuitive knowing will provide us with all we need to continue our journey.

Suggested Reflection Process ꙮ

One of the ways to access intuitive insight is to write or draw with your nondominant hand. When you do this, you bypass your more dominant patterns of judgment and the truth is better able to surface. Select one of the themes below (or one of your own), and explore it with your nondominant hand:

*   The intuitive place inside of me looks like . . .

*   I am so ashamed when I feel . . .

*   Sometimes I just can't explain it, but I *know* . . .

When you sense that your intuitive insight or feelings are blocked, you might find it helpful to choose a new media of expression. If you use dance for your prayer or expression, experiment with writing; if you often paint, then try music or poetry.

8. Integrity

Living in Truth

*A*lthough we innately know the truth, we may, at times, have difficulty naming it. If we listen to our heart and gut, however, we eventually will hear the voice of integrity. It may be blanketed with messages of guilt, buried under patterns of lies, or dulled with denial, but the whisper of truth remains. Invariably, along our soul-journey, we will struggle to know that sense of integrity, longing to be faithful to our deepest self. During these times, we seek the voice of our spirit that speaks with inner authority.

When we become so layered with the "right ways" to think, act, live, and believe, we can easily lose touch with the truth that is truly ours. Some of these layers have been with us a long time, often since childhood. We may have been told, for example, that there is only one way to do something, while being discouraged from exploring other options. Perhaps we had deep feelings or insights that were never expressed because it was deemed inappropriate. Shame, fear of being unacceptable, attempts to please others or earn love: all seem to lead us to question or doubt our own truth. The expectations of our family, our society, and our religion can make it difficult for us to trust the voice of our heart, let alone act with integrity.

True integrity grows from an awareness that we can, in fact, stand in the honest light of God's unconditional love and be seen in our truth. Knowing that, dare we be honest with ourselves and release the lies that inhabit our heart? Integrity, like a muscle, needs to be worked and stretched. Daily we must practice truth-telling in the sacred space of our heart as we name without judgment what we see and feel and know. It is a discipline of faithfulness that calls us to come home to our authentic self.

The path to an honest heart is often difficult as we tangle with the jungle-like growth of our inner critic and the old voices of shame that are so deeply rooted within. Because we have become comfortable with our lies, often fooling even ourselves, the going may be slow and painstaking as we cut away all that is not authentic. Only when we sit with God, the core of truth, can we move through the muck and swamp of our confusion. There we ask for patience, clarity, and trust that we will be given ears to hear the truth and an open heart to hold it.

As we sit in this center of integrity, our heart and God's heart beat as one. The transparent light of truth filters through, embracing every cell of our being, and we are able to see and speak more clearly. Then, little by little, as the layers of lies and pretending are stripped aside, a genuine simplicity remains. Freed of grandiosity and illusion, we stand radiant and unencumbered in truth as we claim our own voice with which we dare speak our truth and live with integrity.

Suggested Reflection Process ✗

Standing in integrity often requires that we remove many layers before we come to that center of truth. Choose a process that will require pulling back numerous coverings or layers. As you remove each layer, begin naming the lies, fears, or illusions that prevent you from walking in integrity. Clay lends itself well to this process, or you may try painting layers around a photo or a simple drawing of yourself.

Look at the ways you disguise your true self. What masks do you wear? What do those masks look like? Draw or make a mask that reflects the disguise you wear to hide your true self.

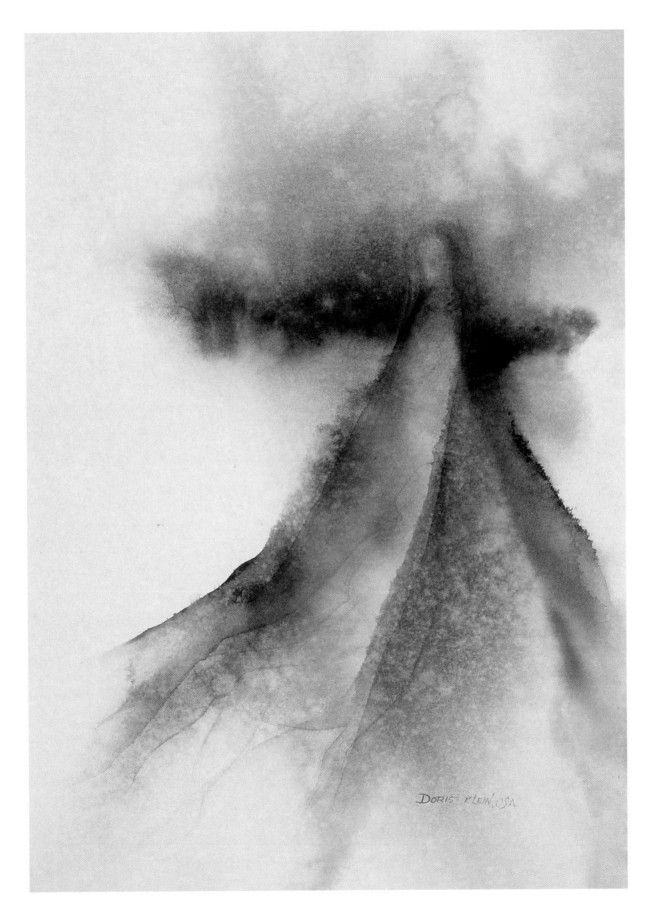

9. Leaning into Letting Go

Befriending Loss

*L*etting go is not exactly what most of us relish. The process generally asks that we move from a place of comfort or knowing to a place of newness that can be uncomfortable and filled with questions and uncertainty. Paradox seems palpable as we take in the many ramifications of this time of passage. We are called to recognize that letting go is a multilayered process of facing and naming the many emotions, fears, and truths that surround us. It is a time when we need to walk slowly through each piece of the process without shame, to grapple with change, and to confront our illusion and fear that we will die if we let go. We long to believe that God supports us in this process even as we feel helpless and alone.

Along the pathways of our lives, we have seen the many faces of letting go. Perhaps we've seen the face of letting go in the death of someone we love. Suddenly or through a lengthy illness, we were challenged to loosen our grip and allow our loved one to move into a new way of being, leaving us behind. Some of us have seen the face of letting go in a relationship that changed or disappeared from our lives completely, by circumstance or choice. And there are those of us who see the face of letting go in the failing of our own physical abilities, as we move into a place of greater dependence on others. The list is endless and colored by the stories of our life.

Honesty, patience, and trust are vital in all phases of letting go. The ability to name honestly our resistance requires that we affirm and recall the larger, loving Presence that holds us here. Although we feel so alone, somehow we need to acknowledge in trust the Love that supports us here. For sure, it is a slow walk through the process, and we sometimes are tempted to run quickly through each layer in an effort to avoid the pain. When we do, however, we are called back to look again at what we missed the first time through.

To face our letting go in honesty touches all levels of our knowing. Sometimes we can list all the rational facts of change. We say things like, "Of course it's time to move on," "She will be in a better place," or "I know that I need to change this pattern in my life." We have been well versed in this language, and we know the acceptable, appropriate explanations. But to know the full reality of letting go, we must name the paradoxes that bubble below the surface. While we know it's "time to move on," we must also name that we don't want to or that we are afraid to, and why. To face this deliberate and conscious naming without judgment becomes our challenge, aware that our patterns of shame often rise as we attempt to wrestle the truth free.

At other times, the change is perceived as irrational and unexplainable. We declare, "This never should have happened!" "I don't understand why!" "I shouldn't have to let go!" "I don't want to!" Anger surfaces at our inability to understand and be in control—and it is so hard to give a voice to this rage. Once again, the integrity of our emotions is often stuffed as we resist naming the deeply held feelings. Can we face these feelings, name the rage, and confront the fear, terror, and profound sadness beneath it? As each feeling arises we are invited to move through the layers, to resist our patterns of denying, ignoring, or shaming, and to be attentive to the truth they carry in our heart.

To let go is to face a place of emptiness that feels eternal. The process beckons us to believe that in this seemingly barren and isolated place, we are never alone. Dare we trust that there is a compassionate Presence that companions us here? Can we lean into the process of letting go, knowing that we are supported even when we feel so empty?

Our prayer of leaning into letting go is a simple plea to trust that this emptiness will make way for fullness as we lean into this space. We ask to believe that we can face this time or circumstance and have what we need to be faithful. Mostly, our prayer of leaning into letting go is a deep breath that simply allows us to acknowledge that we have no answers. We watch and wait and simply ask to know that we are loved.

Suggested Reflection Process ⤳

Notice the larger figure-like form in this painting: this figure images the Mystery of God and the call to let go. A figure, painted in very subtle tones, appears to be gingerly leaning into the Mystery.

In a seated position, assume a similar pose, leaning into a stable object (such as a wall, a piece of furniture, or the side of a hill). Consciously feel your body supported by whatever you're sitting on or leaning against. So often we hold our body muscles tightly, failing to allow ourselves to be supported by whatever is beneath us.

Spend a few moments taking several deep breaths and grounding yourself. When you feel ready, reflect on one of your experiences of letting go. Retell the story to yourself, and recall the feelings that surround that experience. If you are in a safe and private space, you may find it helpful to speak out loud. Name any fears, apprehensions, anger, or sadness. If you have no words, simply image the time and feel your body leaning into the supporting surface, remaining mindful of the larger, supportive Presence of the Holy who companions you in this process.

When you finish, take several deep breaths, and spend a few moments stretching out and feeling your feet on the ground. Walking and other body movement are important elements of letting go. Choose some activity (walking, dance, or stretching) that facilitates moving through this layered process.

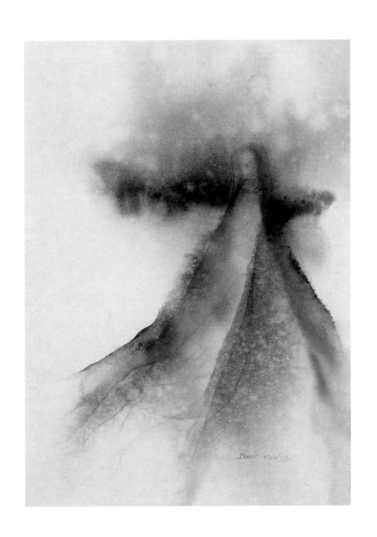

誕生の時、先代の祖母達が
そこにいて下さった

10. The Grandmothers Were There When You Were Brought Forth

Gathering Our Ancestors

*B*loodlines are our sacred connections to the wisdom of our ancestors. Each of us has been touched by the hands and hearts of generations of women from whom we have been born. Our lineage to these mothers and grandmothers links us to the energy, passion, and wisdom they carry.

In addition to our physical ancestors, we also have many other soul-connections to those maternal companions who have loved us into life. It is a gift to tap into the sometimes forgotten resource of their inspiration, hope, and wisdom that supports us on our journey.

As our path unfolds, we continuously give birth to ourselves since, as our life changes, we discover new ways of being and knowing. Sometimes, when confronted with situations for which we feel unprepared, we will seek the insight, guidance, and wisdom of others who have become our trusted companions. When these trusted companions, for whatever reasons, are suddenly gone or cannot be with us, however, we often panic, fearing we are left alone.

It was at just such a time that I painted this piece. In the midst of a major change in my life, I felt as if I were holding a newborn in my arms without anyone around, and I feared I did not know what to do. As I painted that image, the pigment began to yield the figures of many others who seemed to crowd around me in support. Gradually—and to my surprise—the procession grew, and I perceived many ancestors, even soul-companions from distant lands, standing with me in that transformative time. As I defined each figure, I realized that I was not alone but, in fact, was supported by a long line of grandmother-like soul-companions. As the distance of time and geography melted into an awareness of their presence, and as a reminder of our connections to all life-givers throughout the world, I painted the title in Japanese calligraphy: "The Grandmothers Were There When You Were Brought Forth."

The painting suggests an image of each of us seated alone in an expansive, warmly lit cave into which we invite all who have helped give birth to our spirit. One by one, they enter in silence, walking to the rhythm of our heartbeat. As each pauses before us, we simply connect with a glance of gratitude, thanking them for the gifts they have brought. As our mother, grandmothers, and great-grandmothers silently approach us, we thank each of them for the gift of life they have passed on to us, remembering and greeting, too, all the women and men who raised us and met our physical needs as we were growing up.

In this procession, we also acknowledge those individuals who have parented us in places left untended. Here we meet our soul-companions, those nurturing mentors, guides, and healers who tenderly heard and reverently held the stories of our heart. We honor the many ways they taught us to companion ourselves as we grew to stand on our own feet in integrity and walk in grace. These are those soul-mothers of our spiritual bloodline who have connected us to the Sacred, awakening our hearts to the Holy. They are joined by our friends whose support, laughter, listening, and love have brought us delight, wholeness, and healing.

Finally, we invite the poets, painters, musicians, and mystics to enter this cave of our heart. With gratitude, we honor the ways they have touched our deepest spirit and have encouraged us to speak with our own creative voice. Also joining the ancestral dance are those figures of our religious traditions, the sacred companions who have modeled for us the genuine meaning of faithfulness.

The procession is completed with the entrance of the divine One who stands before us in love. It is this Presence of the Holy that confirms in us the goodness in which we were born and the goodness that we continue to bring to birth in our world. Here we are asked to open our hearts in gratitude and hold in every cell of our being the truth that, never alone, we are continually held in the loving cave of the Heart of our God.

Suggested Reflection Process

Sitting in a quiet, dimly lit setting where you can be alone, use the image shared above and allow the procession of your soul-companions to unfold in your heart. Invite the ancestors of your life and spirit to stand with you in a scared place as you thank them for the many ways you are companioned.

Choose various creative ways to explore this image. You may wish to dance with the circle of ancestors, write a litany of gratitude, or paint or draw the procession. Find your voice of gratitude as you recall these soul-companions and the support they continue to bring you.

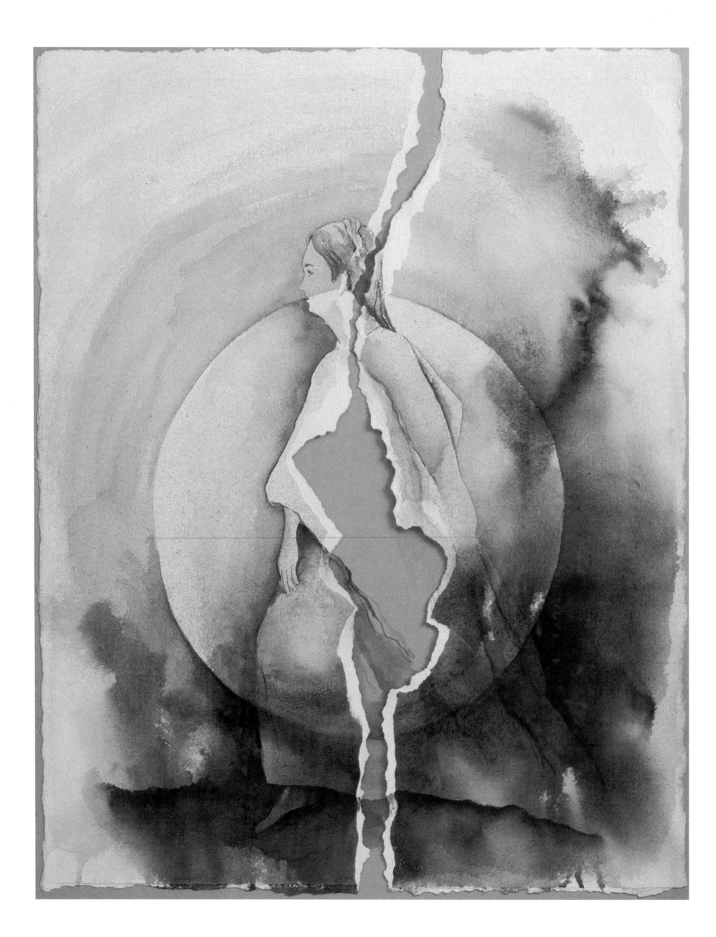

11. The Torn Woman

Walking with the Tears
in the Fabric of Life

*I*t's amazing how many people see this painting, say, "I know her," and then proceed to tell a story of a tear in the fabric of their life. Sometimes the story is about an illness or a death. At other times, the image speaks of a break or betrayal in a relationship. Viewers often are reminded of the brokenness of their own weakness and unfaithfulness. The stories are as endless as those who walk into the image and recount the torn experiences of their soul-journey.

This painting was done during a time of emptiness and turmoil. I had recently lost one of the most nurturing figures in my life and, devastated, I hadn't painted for months. I actually feared that there was no inspiration left in my soul and spirit. In addition to my personal grief, the Gulf War was raging and seemed to be tearing apart the lives of women, children, and men, even the earth herself.

In an effort to translate some of this grief, I purchased a large sheet of expensive watercolor paper, believing that surely I could do a good painting if I had good paper. When I put on the initial wash of color, however, the browns, blues, and purples looked like a muddy mess—and in less than three minutes I had ruined my costly paper. Attempting to salvage something of the work, I painted around a circle that I laid in the middle of the sheet. When I lifted the circle, a space remained that resembled the earth. Looking at the

The Torn Woman

composition, I said out loud, "My life's a mess! The world's a mess! This painting's a mess!" I picked up the sheet, tore it in half, slapped the two torn pieces onto my table, and said, "Doris, you are angry!" (Funny, we are often the last to know!) I then attached the pieces to a larger sheet, leaving a space between them where I began to paint the woman. Finally, when I finished the work and hung it for viewing, a deep quiet came over me.

It's amazing how afraid we are to name and be with the torn places of our lives. Our pattern is often one of denial as we attempt to avoid the pain and the truth. At some of those moments, our most common responses are: "I'm falling apart." "I can't keep it together!" "I'm coming undone!" Instead of facing the facts and feelings of our brokenness, we often hide or deny them, fearing they might destroy us. We are afraid that if we are seen in this place, we will be left; if others *really* know us they will go away. In fact, we may enter so deeply into this broken space as to fear that even God cannot love us. Here, as we fall into self-hatred and disgust at our weakness, we even abandon ourselves.

There is hope in this painting, however, in that the figure is not hiding or collapsed but boldly walking with the tear. She appears to be held together by a larger, unseen energy that empowers her as she walks ahead, focused on something greater than her wound. The image carries the reminder that there is a loving Presence who sees us in our truth and companions us as we face the tears of our body, mind, and spirit. It is only in faith that we believe God walks with the torn man and the torn woman in each of us.

Some of our torn experiences find us quickly upright and walking on in faith. At other times, however, we struggle with the process, believing that we must go here alone, that alone we must hold it together. We forget to ask to know the companionship and unconditional love of the Divine. We forget to listen for that still and reassuring voice: "I know you. I knit you together in your mother's womb"(see Psalm 139). Dare we trust that we can be seen and loved in these places of weakness and despair? Will not the same God who knit us together in the womb continue to knit together the tears of our lives? Can we believe that God walks with the torn woman or the torn man in each of us, that God walks with the people of our torn nations and world?

Suggested Reflection Process ✍

Tear a full sheet of paper lengthwise down the center, and paste or tape both pieces to a second sheet of paper, leaving space between the torn pieces. On the second sheet of paper, begin writing or drawing, allowing your expressions to overlap on the torn pieces as well as fill the space between them. Let the words and images lead you into the experiences and feelings of the tears in your life.

Describe what you look like in your torn places. You may choose to write, paint, sing, or use some kind of body movement to give voice to this description. This is a process of naming not fixing. Once completed, bless the expression with a symbol of God. You might simply light a candle, speak the name of the Divine, or add paint to your image, with the intention of remembering that you are seen in this place with compassion, support, and love.

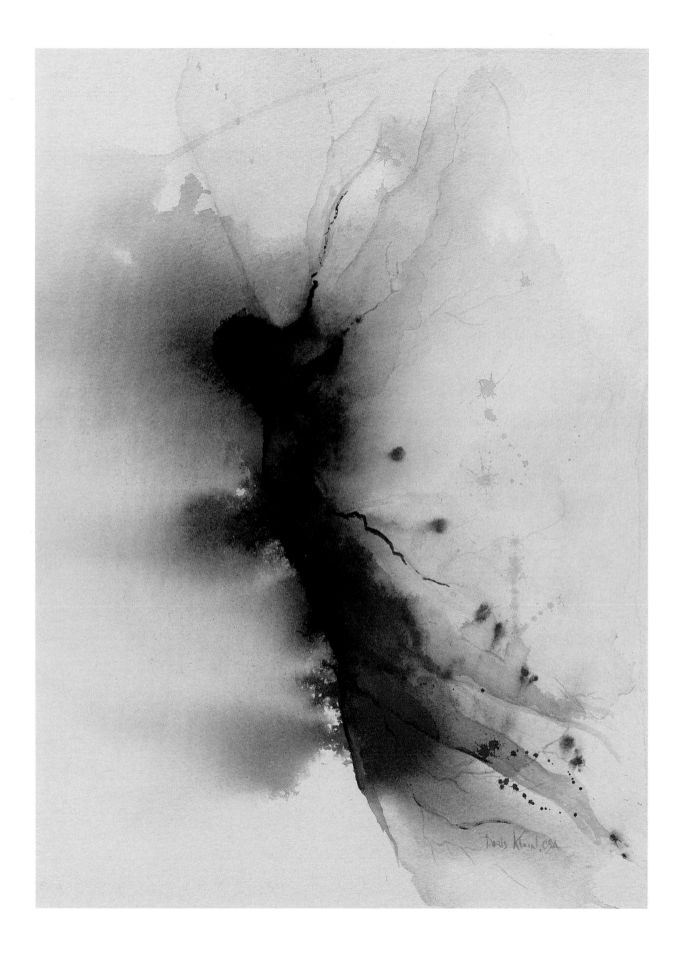

12. Transformation

Moving through Change

$\mathcal{T}$he paradox of transformation is the paradox of death/resurrection, a time of dying to what was as we move into what will be. It is a strange mix of color and darkness, of knowing and unknowing, as we face the multiple transitions and changes of life.

I was in the midst of one of these times when I painted this piece. One of my dearest friends was dying, and I was straddling that awkward place between my faith and my feelings. I imaged the hope of the freedom that was before her as I randomly splashed bright swatches of color on the paper. Although I was aware of the hope-filled teachings of resurrection and eternal life, I also was keenly aware of the deep hues of my grief and unwillingness to let go.

As I touched those feelings, I loaded a brush with dark-blue and black pigment and, with frustration, confusion, and anger, I slathered it next to the brilliant color. Realizing that both were true, I sprayed the piece with a mist of water and the colors began to separate and blend at the same time. As they moved, I began to recognize in the piece the profile of a person angled between the contrasting colors, legs and arms seeming to explode into wings of flight. The image, like a candid photograph of an unsuspecting soul, seemed to capture the transformative journey both my friend and I were beginning as we moved with and into the Mystery of God. These transformative moments find us suspended in a place where we must let go and leap into the unknown. Here we face the changes and sometimes even the death of our hopes, our dreams, our bodies, and our relationships.

The grace of transformation is the gift to trust that all things will be well as new ways of being and living arise from the ashes. We can't pretend to understand the paradox as we stand in the midst of change; we grasp neither the immensity of the challenge nor the immensity of the Love that sustains us in this transforming process. While it does not make sense to our linear mind, we are invited to trust in the merciful God who supports us in this suspended place, giving us all we need to lift the wings of our heart.

Trust does not minimize the terror we know as we make these passages of transition. In fact, our feelings are very real and must be honored in truth rather than ignored in judgment and denial. If we fail to face these emotions in truth, the heat of harbored rage will destroy us, and the weight of unvoiced sadness will sink us into despair. These voices of our soul demand honest acknowledgment and release if we are to move beyond the pain.

This is a solitary journey. Although we wish others could be with us in this passage, we must claim our own solitary transition as we face the call to let go and move on in faith. Although we are surrounded with companions and witnesses, we alone can know the secrets of our soul as we move along our own transformative journey. Our task is to compassionately stay with ourselves in this passage through paradox, mindful that we need simply ask to trust as we surrender into the breath of God who holds us together here, making all things new.

Suggested Reflection Process ⟩⟩

Take a few moments to recall some of your own times of transformation. Choose a specific experience or current transition, and use pigments, movement, music, or words to paint a picture of the passage. Gradually name all the levels of letting go, even the ones you would rather ignore or deny. This is not an effort to come to an answer or conclusion but simply an attempt to describe your times of transformation as you identify the many voices of your soul on this journey to newness. Allow the process to unfold, knowing that you may need to repeat phrases, movements, melodies, or patterns until you and they become more comfortable.

Stop periodically and breathe as you sit with your creative expression—without judgment or shame—simply being with the truth it holds. Conclude segments or the completion of the process with a simple gesture of prayer, asking for trust in this time of transformation.

13. Dance of Delight

Living with Joy

*O*ur multiple commitments often find us intensely engaged in the tasks of life. With focused integrity, we become the helpers, holders, and healers of the world. We take care of everyone—we even try to take care of God! This mission is approached with utmost dedication and the seriousness it deserves. After all, we and our world are faced with many challenges and adversities as we walk this life path. Unfortunately, we often assume a degree of self-sufficiency and sophistication as we take control and direct all of our intensity to the tasks of service. Amid the "all business" attitude, we begin to seriously believe that the success or failure of each project depends on us—and we become even more intense.

I believe we are seen in this process by a gentler, calmer Presence who places a tender hand on our cheek and says to each of us, "Thank you! Thank you for working so hard! Thank you for being so good. Thank you for being so organized and efficient. Thank you for demanding excellence and quality. Thank you for bringing sustenance to so many in need. Thank you for your time, your energy, your intensity, your dedication, your enthusiasm." Perhaps that hand then gently pats us on the cheek and says, "Now give it a rest, Honey! Lighten up!"

At times, we are taken in by the lie that unless it's hard or painful it can't possibly be of God. We are certain that ever since that "apple incident" in Eden, the infinite presence and power of the Holy demands and expects unending work, pain, and struggle. We forget that we were created in blessing and called to live in light. Perhaps one of our greatest challenges in faith is the challenge to laugh and enjoy. Our imagery often layers God with severity, judgment, and retribution. Dare we believe that we are made to mirror a joyous God who delights in laughter, beauty, and pleasure? We are called by this Creator and Companion to balance the reality of our pain with the generously provided gifts of pleasure.

We often link the struggles of our soul-journey with a serious assent to sanctity, seldom counting among our sins the failure to laugh and simply delight in the gifts of life. Our work ethic is often applied to our spiritual life, as our prayer becomes a task to be completed rather than an enjoyment to be savored. At times, even the obligations of religion become life-sapping rather than life-giving, as we get stuck in the demands of duty and detail. We must continually call ourselves and our faith communities to authentic worship that touches the integrity of the God of light and joy.

Our restless hearts long to rest in the delight and pure pleasure of the Divine. By no means is this an invitation to construct false fronts of denial or patterns of pretending but, rather, to develop a discipline of balance. We are invited to lighten our spirits as we relax into the Arms of Light, knowing that even amid our struggle we are given a heart that was created to dance with joy.

Suggested Reflection Process ⟫

Take some time to reflect on balance in your life. Begin by imaging the hand of the Holy on your cheek, thanking you for all your goodness. Make a list or speak out loud all of your qualities and "accomplishments." List and affirm the many ways you are of service to others.

Next, reflect on the balancing ways you celebrate life. How do you relax and have fun? What brings you delight? What simple joys renew you? With whom can you share these joys? Again, write these down or speak them out loud. Conclude by creating something that will remind you to "lighten up!" It might be a mantra, a sign, or a piece of music that will help you develop a discipline of balance.

14. *Waiting*

Trusting the Process

*B*usy with other things, I hadn't painted for nearly a year. Finally, I had a hiatus and found time just to paint. I presumed I'd be prolific, of course, and why not? I had no distractions, no excuses, no reasons, not to roll up my sleeves and begin—but when I did, there was nothing there. There was no inspiration, no insight. It was a strange and uncomfortable struggle as I wondered what I was doing wrong. By comparison, it seemed that everyone around me was profitably occupied and productive.

In my struggle to describe this awkward experience to a small group of sacred companions one rainy evening, a dear friend among them named this vulnerable, naked time as *waiting*. He invited me to breathe, to be patient, to allow the sound of the rain to gently quiet my panic and fear.

The following day, when I tried to translate the experience from the previous evening, I drew a reclining nude, but her head didn't fit at the bottom of a large sheet of paper, where I had positioned the figure. I erased the whole thing and started over—but again, the figure's head didn't fit. Of course! What I was trying to hold in my *head* was, in fact, a process of my *heart* and *body*. There were no words to explain this vulnerable place of waiting in mystery.

It's quite amazing how we have come to link our value and worth with our productivity and performance. Because we so often become what we do, we tend to question our value and merit in times of inactivity. And, understandably, there is a vulnerable nakedness in these waiting times. We fear that we are loved only for what we do, and find it hard to trust that we can be loved for who we are. As the discomfort of this time unfolds, our patience runs thin. We are so programmed and driven to be productive that when, for various reason, we can't produce, we panic. Suddenly we realize that the chaos of our busyness has become the garment of our self-definition. Now what?

The discomfort that seems to pursue us during this time comes not so much from outside of us but from those well-learned messages within that challenge our worth in this less active stance. We hear those old mental tapes judging this inactivity as somehow wrong, and we attempt something—anything—to fill the space with "doing." We compare ourselves to others and their busyness, certain that we somehow are "less than" because of our inactivity. We simply presume that nothing is happening when, in fact, some of our most profound and immeasurable development is taking place in the quiet within. Of course, we wonder as we wait: "Why is it taking so long? Something should be happening by now! What am I doing wrong? How can I fix this—fast?"

We each know this waiting experience. Perhaps it's waiting for clarity amid confusion and chaos; perhaps it's waiting to know the right decision. A friend saw this painting and tearfully said, "I'm waiting to pray."

The experience is not unlike that of being pregnant. Our bodies teach us the wisdom of tenderly holding new life within as we wait for it to grow, develop, and be born. In the same way, we need to hold and nurture our hopes, dreams, and ideas, waiting for them to come to full term. We grow in trust as we discover that these periods of apparent inactivity are often some of our most generative times. Soul-work is being done as the Creator conceives newness in the silence within and we prepare to give birth as we wait.

Suggested Reflection Process ✆

Clear a space of all distractions, and sit or lie in that space. If your time is limited, set a timer so you don't have to watch the clock. Turn off radios, phones, beepers, or anything that will interrupt the silence.

In a comfortable sitting or lying position, take several deep breaths. Sink into whatever surface you are resting on, allowing it to support you. Consciously breathe into each part of your body, and allow each exhalation to take with it any tension or tightness. Focus your attention on simply being right where you are, and let go of any judgments about what else you should be doing. Your task for the next few minutes is simply to *be*. You may want to image yourself resting in a place that brings you calm and comfort.

In this position of resting, be aware of a presence of the Holy that simply waits with you. How does God affirm you here? What words are spoken to your heart? Can you simply *be* in this position and recognize you are loved for who you are? What do you ask for in this waiting time?

You may want to follow this imagery with some timed writing or other creative expression.

15. The Midwives

Witnessing Transition

I recently visited a friend who asked to trace the outline of my hand on a piece of fabric; she was making a quilt designed to celebrate and remember significant individuals who had touched her life. As she created the piece, stitching the design of each hand, she was able to recount in gratitude the many ways she had been loved and supported. It was a comforting image to know that, once completed, she would be able to wrap up in this quilt, surrounding herself with a tactile reminder of her soul-companions. Even when separated by distance or death, the connection to the touch of those loving hands and hearts would continue. This material reminder held the energy and support of those many midwives of her life.

Each of us has been touched by the hands and hearts of soul-companions who have walked with us as we faced times of transition—times of passages when we experienced the births and deaths of our body, mind, and spirit. Although we alone can walk through those times of change, God surrounds us with midwives who assist us in the process of walking through those torn places. The ancestors who have gone before us, as well as the soul-companions walking beside us, are the midwives who support and encourage us in this process of movement and change.

In the physical birthing process, the midwife attends to the needs of the mother, often inviting her to breathe as she experiences the pains of delivery. The midwife's voice supports and challenges the mother to focus her energy, reminding her of the new life that is about to emerge. Those who companion people in their dying process play a similar role. They, too, encourage their patient to breathe through the difficulty of letting go as they lean into the Mystery that awaits. Yet between these two major events are many other birthing and dying moments, moments when we are touched by the loving support of others. Our midwives during those times are those who remind us to breathe, who help us stay focused on the mystery of our transition time. They challenge us to be faithful to our truth, and they encourage us to walk in trust. Sometimes they simply stand with us as wordless witnesses to our joy, pain, and passage.

When we stand before the torn openings of life, we face the unknown. Alone, we make the journey through this space of Mystery but, like the figure in this painting, we are surrounded by a circle of midwives, those soul-companions who stand with us in our sacred places of change. The figures faintly pictured around the tear are those witnesses we may have never seen, our ancestors or the poets, authors, artists, and mystics whose work has met us in these soul-moments. Others around us in these times are quite clear. We know them by name. We have felt the encouraging touch of their hands and words amid our passage experiences.

There also are times on this journey when we are called upon to midwife others, to be willing to stand with compassion as we companion them through transition times. Saint Teresa of Avila reminds us that Christ has no body now but ours. We must be those hands that gently touch and firmly encourage others as our eyes mirror God's compassion to them.

Whether facing our own times of passage or witnessing the transitions of others, we are reminded that the holy One is faithfully there beside us, prompting us to breathe, reminding us we are not alone. The divine Midwife will not leave our side and will be joined by others who mirror her love.

Suggested Reflection Process ⟫

Take some time to recount the midwives in your life. As you reflect on times of transition and change, who were your supportive companions? Who are those soul-companions who stand in the sacred spaces of your journey and witness the spiritual challenges and passages of your life? Translate your reflection by writing a litany of gratitude, naming your midwives. You may want to create a mantra-like response as you bless each soul-companion.

Take time to recount the occasions you have been midwife to others. Again, in a litany format, be thankful for the gifts you were given that enabled you to stand with others along their way.

16. Tenderness

Nurturing Our Spirit

*I*n awe of the miracle of life, we readily respond to a newborn infant. How clearly the experience of holding a child teaches us the vital role of nurturing one so totally dependant on others. In the presence of an infant, we quickly set aside the sophistication of role or education and extend the natural touch of tenderness. Our entire being seems to magically open as we find ways to meet the child's needs, calm the child's fears, and nourish the child's body and spirit—in other words, express our unconditional love to this little one.

This kind of gentleness is not unlike the tenderness we desire ourselves, a longing that may stem from unmet needs of the past when we, ourselves, were deprived of touch and nurturing support. Our search for this tenderness, especially in our adult life, can lead us to hope that somehow the emptiness of long ago can be filled with relationships or things—thus satisfying that gnawing inner desire. When we live with the illusion that the satisfaction is beyond our reach, however, we fail to recognize that we must meet *our own* deepest need to be loved.

All of us, no matter what our history, are called to befriend and nurture our own spirit. When Jesus spoke about how we are to love others, he clearly reminded us that it was to be as we love ourselves. Yet, our efforts to avoid the sins of selfishness have sometimes blinded our vision to the responsibility we have to tender our own heart, care for our own body, and nurture our own spirit.

Tenderness

It's quite amazing how the metaphors we have used for God can influence us in this experience. When we were young children, our parents were mirrors of God, since they held the power to meet our needs and thus be responsible for our survival. If we were aware of their unconditional nurturing love and firm, direct guidance, then they taught us well of the divine One. If, however, the images we developed for God drew heavily on a critical, punishing, parental presence, that harsh voice continues to echo in our hearts today.

How would our life be different if we believed we were tenderly held in the loving embrace of a gentle nurturing God who loves us as we are no matter what? Can we take in Isaiah's metaphor of a mother comforting a child (see Isaiah 66:13)? In our adult sophistication, we lose sight of our need for that nurturing embrace of unconditional love. We become so focused on being the helpers, holders, and healers in our world that we forget the God who helps, holds, and heals us. Sometimes, caught in our patterns of shame or remembered abandonment, we resist leaning into the abundant lap of God, fearing we will be disappointed. Dare we believe that we are looked upon by this divine Parent and are simply loved for who we are?

As we experience more clearly this loving, tender God, we become more loving and tender with ourselves, and from this grounded connection with Love, we are able to extend that love and compassion to others. In this process we discover healthy ways to meet our own needs, calm our own fears, and nourish our own body and spirit.

Suggested Reflection Process

Walk into the painting and allow yourself to be the infant, dependent on the softer, larger, loving presence of God. You may find it helpful to sit in a rocker, wrap up in a blanket, or hold a pillow as you image being embraced by Love. Speak out loud the comforting, supporting, and encouraging words you long to hear and may often offer to others. Listen attentively to your own heart. Be gentle and understanding with yourself. If you have no words, try listening to quieting music. (I highly recommend Shaina Noll's *Songs for the Inner Child*, especially "How Could Anyone Ever Tell You, You Were Anything Less Than Beautiful.")

At the conclusion of your reflection, write a topical poem or a mantra that you can return to when you need to be reminded of this nurturing Love.

17. Simplicity

Uncluttering Our Life

*W*e often are convinced that if we are to be truly happy, we need certain possessions, power, relationships, or roles. Setting out to gather these lures into our life, we find ourselves confused and disillusioned about our choices of objects, positions, or actions that falsely portray happiness. Invariably, we find these things hollow, unable to provide us with the results we were looking for. Thus, it serves us well to pause in our society of accumulation so that we can unearth that which genuinely supports a pure place of inner delight and fullness.

The essentials of completeness are buried beneath layers of clutter that prevent us from knowing the freedom and delight we long for. Among that clutter is the conviction that "getting this" or "doing that" or "becoming something" will make us happy. The perspective of our shame urges us to grasp at anything that will make us feel okay. Instead of facing our insecurity and claiming our own inner authority—instead of naming that inner emptiness— we grasp at position and power, believing they will make us feel fulfilled, satisfied.

Consumerism also contributes to that clutter. Consumerism toys with our mind as we are daily barraged with media messages attempting to convince us that we will be happy only if we have a certain product. Our competitive society constantly places us in a mode of seeking to "have more than" or "be better than" others, implying that "having more" or "being better" will make us complete and whole. It is this addictive enticement that deters us from grappling with the deeper questions and challenges of simplicity.

Simplicity

For many of us, our daily busyness is part of the clutter as well. We try to keep ourselves constantly engaged in the noise of activity, for example, so we won't have to sit with the truth in our heart. Sometimes even our pain becomes the clutter, as we focus on the multiple wounds of our body and spirit while avoiding the questions those wounds suggest we raise. At times, we attempt to cling to past relationships, events, or memories by accumulating items that we associate with these things. As a result, the rich ritual of remembering becomes just one more piece of clutter that we cling to in an attempt to avoid our fear of letting go and moving on into the future. The clutter is endless as we each look at our own patterns of accumulation and avoidance.

It is not uncommon for us to lose track of what is essential and thus miss the simple pleasures we were meant to enjoy. We are challenged to begin the process of sorting through the clutter that is *literally* in our closets or *figuratively* in our hearts, clearing paths to truth, beauty, and genuine treasures. As we examine and name our sins of accumulation and greed, we come face to face with our fears and the many ways we have learned to deceive ourselves. Can we identify what is enough from our places of too much? Are we so accustomed to the clutter in our lives that we have grown to believe it is essential to our survival? Only when we are willing to ask these demanding questions can we recognize that what we have sought so diligently from outside can be truly discovered only from within.

But how do we define the essentials in our life? Can we, in fact, freely choose to graciously begin letting go of the nonessentials that clutter our heart? Can we rest with confidence in the promise of our God who assures us that we will be given all we need? Yes, for emptiness makes way for fullness. Perhaps we have personally experienced or have heard stories of others who, through some tragedy, lost everything. Amid this kind of grief comes an awareness of what is, in fact, essential.

Simplicity

Indeed, it is a risk—letting go of all the clutter we use to provide ourselves with a false sense of security and worth. Yet, we were made to be happy, to delight in the beauty and the wonder of ourselves, one another, and our earth. As we attempt to walk more simply, we are challenged to assume a stance of gracefully sharing all that we have, to be attentive to what is essential, to unclutter our lives and open our hearts to create an emptiness where fullness becomes possible. The paradox of the beatitudes reminds us that emptiness makes way for fullness, that poverty provides abundance.

Suggested Reflection Process ⟩⟩

Choose an area where you accumulate clutter. This might be a desk drawer, a closet, or an entire room. (Don't bite off too much!) Pray your way through the accumulation as you consciously sort through, give away, discard, and simplify this area. Speak your gratitude as you uncover the memories, gifts, and learning you discover there.

Do a timed writing about the clutter in your heart. What do you hold on to that weighs you down or distracts you? Follow the first writing with a second writing focusing on what is underneath the clutter.

18. Lost

Longing for Clarity

Sometimes life is hard! We become tired, confused. We lose our bearings and are unexpectedly upended. Although we struggle to remain in complete control, we are whisked off our feet by a wave of change that leaves us uncertain. We think we have all the answers only to find ourselves suddenly tipped over by an event, a loss, a disappointment. In that moment, what had made perfect sense quickly melts into confusion and uncertainty.

This experience looks different in each of our lives yet, at the same time, we share that universal knowing of darkness and doubt. During these times, we desperately long for certitude, for that certain someone who will have the answer. With noisy questions and demands rattling in our minds, we panic in our search for clarity and a return to that which is calm and familiar. We grasp for anything that might appear to fill the yawning chasm within. And in the midst of it all, we feel so alone, so abandoned. "Now what? Where are the answers? What do I do?"

During these times, we often find ourselves tossed back to that younger place where the fears of the lost child come to the surface. Perhaps we remember actual experiences of being lost, or maybe this occurrence is simply a mirror of the varied ways we knew that alone space in our heart. However the fear might be described, it is a real terror that warns us to be attentive to our own heart. In these experiences, our wise, grounded, adult self must intervene, calming the fears and offering guidance.

Lost

First, we must remember to breathe. Although we may balk at the simplicity of that directive, it is one of our most basic and most essential connections with God. An Aramaic name given to God was the feminine word, *Ruah*, which means "life-sustaining breath." The name portrays a divine Presence whose very breath sustains us and connects us with the rhythm and depth of our own breathing. Dare we believe that God is as close to us as our very breath? When we take the time for deep and rhythmic breathing in the midst of our panic, we can touch again the nearness of God and hear the voice of Ruah, who repeats the mantra of Psalm 46: "Be still, and know that I am God!" It is in that quiet and calming moment that we can turn, in trust, to the larger Love that sustains us here. Breathe!

As we lean into Ruah, we also must feel our feet on the earth and our connection to our deeper knowing. Our panic often takes us to our heads, disconnecting us from the truth we hold in our heart and gut. When we breathe down through our body to our feet on the earth, we are better able to access the clarity for which we had been searching. Although the problems around us remain, we are better able to decipher our way through the confusion. Perhaps the answer we discerned was not what we wanted or expected, but we can rest confident that it will challenge us to even deeper questions.

We continue to recognize that this course of life is a journey, not a destination. Often it is a crooked road, sometimes looping back as we revisit those places that hold more for us to see. What we define as being lost is sometimes our resistance to revisit those places and experiences that challenge our faith and trust. Yet, when we are faithful and honest, we are able to recognize more quickly the landscape of our panic as we remember to breathe and trust that the clarity will follow.

Suggested Reflection Process ⤳

Give yourself a short period of uninterrupted time to simply sit and breathe. (I recommend setting a timer and beginning with a three-minute period.) Breathe in for three counts, breathe out for three counts, and pause for three counts. Repeat the process until the timer sounds. After a few days add a minute to your original time period, and extend your breath another count until you find your natural quieting rhythm. The counting and limited time will help you to focus so that you will not be tempted to divert your attention to other thoughts.

This exercise helps develop a disciple of quiet centering that we can draw on when we lose our balance. Once centered, we are better able to attend to the voice of the Holy within as we discern more the truth and wisdom we carry.

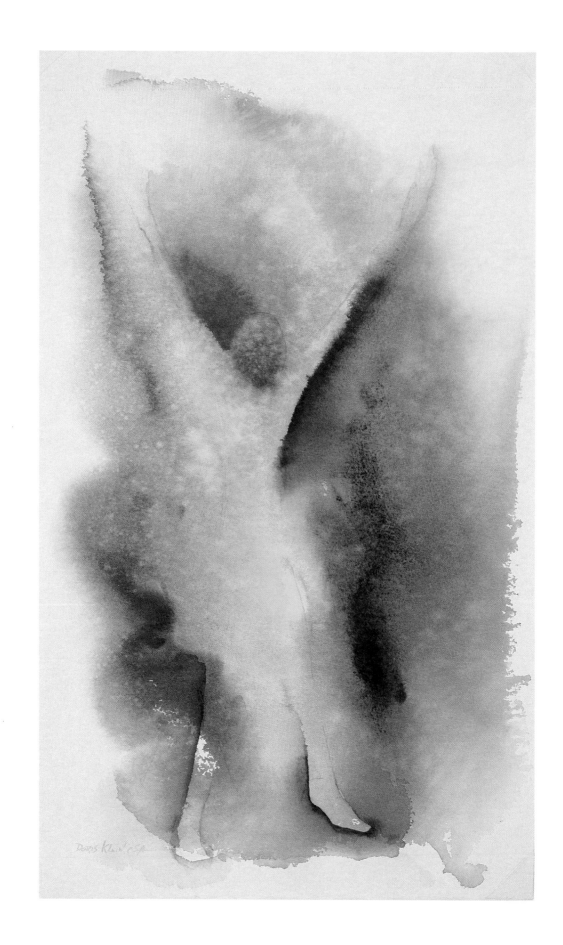

Doris Klein '98

19. Soul-Scream

Giving Voice

*T*here are times when our spirit simply wants to scream out the truth. These are times when we long for the courage to release the cries of our soul as we are confronted with the mysteries of living and loving. Most of us have been taught to hold the multiple feelings that rise within, to give them only proper and socially appropriate expressions. We can carry that learning to an unbalanced place, however, where we fear naming and speaking the truth, even to ourselves. Yet, we must dare to voice the long-held secrets of our soul rather than let them ferment within. We must raise our arms and proclaim what we feel and know in our deepest self.

Unfortunately, layers of shame inhibit us as we avoid the expression of what we really feel, fearing it will actually destroy us. The paradox, in fact, is that the very lack of expression—holding and harboring these feelings—actually becomes the destructive force. When our emotions are held in darkness, they only expand, intensify, and become more difficult to contain and manage. Unattended anger, for example, can become a manipulative passive/aggressive stance as we attempt to get what we think we need from others. Repressed rage can explode in an unguarded moment, wrecking unnecessary havoc. Unnamed sadness can leave us in periods of unexplained crying, or it can push us to grasp at the hearts of others as we try to get the compassion we lack for ourselves. We even forget that our joy, unexpressed, withers for lack of breath and light.

Soul-Scream

Our body, too, pays a price for our failure to give voice to our truth. As we desperately hold on to fear, shame, anxiety, or rage, we tense our muscles, our blood pressure rises, and our heart often breaks in sadness. Even our posture can reflect the heavy secrets of our spirit, as we bend under the weight of unspoken truth.

When we avoid naming and dealing with our deep feelings, we risk being without boundaries, lacking a container sturdy enough to hold all we feel and know. Then, failing to claim what is ours, we recklessly and randomly direct our emotions onto others.

If we can just give voice to these multiple feelings in the home of our heart, we can relate in healthy ways with others. We can achieve a stance of balance and wellness from which we are able to observe and name our feelings without judgment or shame. Many of us need to seek assistance in this process, turning to those soul-companions who will listen as we speak our truth—always remembering that, first and foremost, we need to hear *ourselves*. In this process, we strengthen the container of our self, enabling us to hold what we know.

When we honestly confront these deep feelings and give them voice, we come to know a simpler place that has always been beneath the scream. We strive to be mindful that we can be seen in the truth of our noisy, messy heart and be held in the silent heart of God, where we are quieted and calmed.

Suggested Reflection Process ⅔

I painted this piece when I could find no words for what felt like a volcano of feelings within. What does the wordless place of emotions look like in you? Use crayons or paint, and begin an abstract composition of colors that gives voice to your soul now or as you reflect on a strong emotional experience from your past.

When you finish, pray with your piece of art.

20. Compassion

Companioning Ourselves

*W*e are so good at "being there" for others when they face times of pain, loss, or need. When others we care about are ill, for example, lose a loved one in death, or are faced with a difficult turn in life, our heart reaches out as we graciously stand beside them in supportive compassion. What is often surprising is the difficulty we have staying with ourselves as we encounter similar experiences. We may minimize, deny, mask, or simply ignore the pain that seems to be too much for us to bear. Yet, underneath all the denial, we are so hoping that someone will come and sit with us, listen to our heart, and fix what's broken. We cling to the lie that we would be free of this torment if only someone else would understand. We keep explaining, describing, sometimes exaggerating to others, all the while missing the paradox that *we* need to believe and understand *ourselves*.

There are those times when we attempt to fill this hollow place in our heart with other substances. Telling ourselves that we will feel better if we do this or that only brings us face to face with our addictive patterns. In our attempts to satiate a deeper hunger, we resist staying with ourselves in the moment, where we sit in naked truth.

Eventually, we must face and name without judgment the facts and feelings that are ours. We are the only ones who, with God, can truly hear our heart. Yes, we need outside witnesses and supportive others to companion us but, ultimately, we must sit with ourselves on this dark shore and acknowledge the truths around us. We must be the voice we hear in the night that says, "It's going to be okay. I will stay here with you. I will not abandon you. I will not go away." Then, hearing our own voice, we hear the voice of God's heart as well, reminding us that we continue to be held.

This image is a reflection of our coming to that lonely place within and sitting beside ourselves with wordless compassion, listening to our own heart with understanding and support. It invites us to gently touch the tender places that hurt deeply and say, "There, there. Yes, I hear you. Yes, I understand. Yes, this is really hard, isn't it!" It's not about fixing; rather, it's about naming with compassion our emptiness, our pain, and our deepest places of sadness, fear, and anger.

The figures in the painting are seated on an expansive beach beside a sea that melts into the night. The setting reflects the immense Mystery of God that holds us in our solitary moments of distress. We can compassionately stay with ourselves when we recognize that we are held in the spaciousness of God. Yes, it is often dark, yet we keep learning to trust that we are tenderly held in this vast mystery. Although our well-learned patterns urge us to rush through the pain, we are invited to sit still and be attentive as we mindfully, slowly, gently, listen to our heart's song.

With this loving attention, we touch the compassionate heart of God, who gives us the words our spirit so longs to hear. Judgments melt away in the waves of compassion, and the inner chaos, once given a voice, makes space for the calm to wash in. We continue to ask for the grace to be filled with loving kindness for ourselves, as we extend compassionate kindness to others.

Suggested Reflection Process ✍

As you image yourself seated in this painting, be with the words of Julian of Norwich:

And so our good Lord answered all the questions and doubts I could raise, saying most comfortingly:

> *"I may make all things well, and*
> *I shall make all things well, and*
> *I will make all things well;*
> *and you will see yourself*
> *that every kind of thing shall be well."*[2]

Sit or walk with the mantra, "All shall be well." Repeatedly remind yourself that in times of questioning and doubt, you are companioned by a loving God who can and shall and will make things well. Know that even if at the moment it seems impossible, you, too, "will see yourself that every kind of thing shall be well."

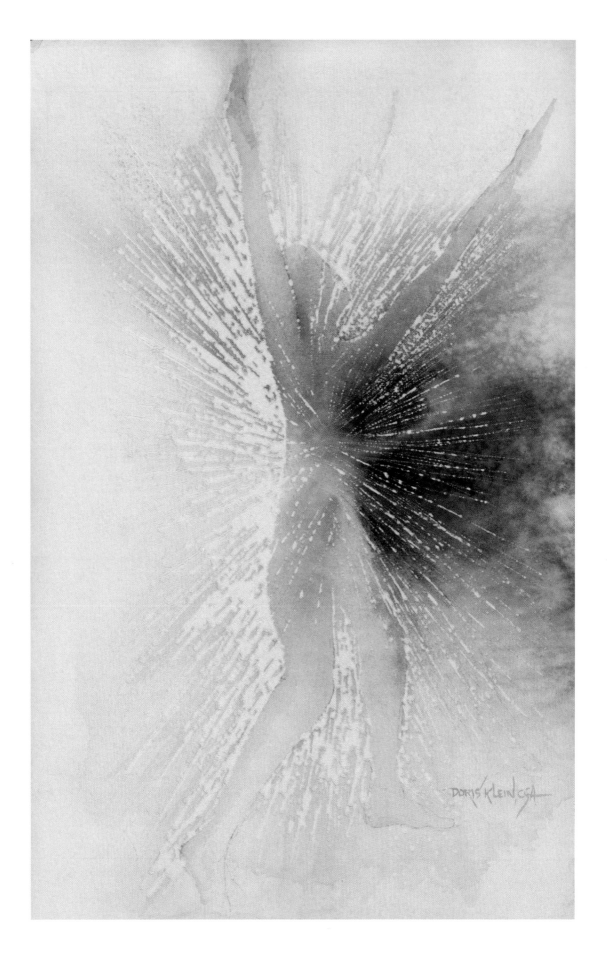

21. Surrender

Letting Go into Love

*W*e often resist using the word surrender because we associate it with the shame and fear of "giving up," "quitting," "failing," and "being defeated." Unfortunately, these negative nuances often distort the richer significance of letting go into love. Surrender actually carries a much richer reality: as we let go, we move into a fullness much greater than we can imagine, a fullness where we receive exactly what we need.

Well schooled in a false sense of control, we usually cling to the illusion of power as we struggle with the paradoxes of life. Each of us knows those times when we dig in our feet, stiffen our body, tighten our jaw, and demand rational explanations for unexplainable events. Granted, we must take an active, assertive stance in our journey of life, making conscious choices from a place of truth and insight. Yet, as we encounter experiences for which there are no answers, no rational explanations or solutions, we arrive at a point where, in faith, we are asked to stand in a Mystery that far exceeds our human understanding.

Surrender seems abstract unless we name our own issues of control. We know, for example, those times when we did all we could, only to find ourselves facing those questions for which there are no linear explanations. Many of us have found ourselves feverishly attempting to hold everything together, trying to control ourselves and everyone else. Perhaps we've known those times when we so wished we could do something, yet we had no resource or recourse; we could only stand by helplessly. The reality is, occurrences, events, or disappointments sometimes leave us helpless, with no answers.

In all of these situations we have choices: we can resist, resent, wrestle, or relax. Convinced we are in charge, we may *resist* letting go, insisting that we simply must try harder to understand or to keep it together. Or *resentment* can permeate our hearts as we struggle with the issues of faith that surround the paradoxes of living and dying. Or we can *wrestle* tenaciously in these times of confusion, clinging to the illusion that our understanding will bring us control. In the resistance, resentment, and wrestling, we can panic and, drained of our energy, demand more and more of ourselves and others.

But the grace of surrender invites us to *relax* into the Mystery, to acknowledge that we cannot walk alone in this place. Rather than assuming a stance of defeat, we ask to be embraced by a Love that is much greater than the confusion, pain, or frustration we are experiencing. We ask for a profound gift when, in the midst of paradox and pain, we pray to stand in surrender. The process of letting go of our challenging and resistance is slow but, little by little, we learn to trust this gift that supports us in our unknowing. Once we accept in our heart the truth of being loved, we loosen our grip on control and are surprisingly free to act in integrity and light.

Rather than submissive defeat, the paradox of letting go into love frees us to walk with renewed life. With our arms raised in naked surrender, we are given an energy that exceeds our greatest hopes and a freedom to walk in joy.

Suggested Reflection Process ⟩

Reflect on a time of struggle in your life. Perhaps you struggled with someone else, an organization or structure, your self, or God. What does it look like when you resist, resent, wrestle, or relax? Answer that question by using one of the following processes:

✳ Write a paragraph describing what you feel, say, and do.

✳ Paint, sculpt, or draw what it looks like or feels like.

✳ Assume a pose, act out, or image a bodily response.

22. Come Home

Releasing Our Shame

One day a face seemed to surface out of a small, abstract wash I was painting. The tentative figure appeared to be wrapped in a blanket or, perhaps, emerging from wet and enfolding wings. The expression on the figure's face seemed cautious, wondering whether to venture forth, if it would be safe to be seen. Her presence led me to reflect on those times of awareness when we recognize the layers of shame that seem to enfold our heart.

So often, we fear being seen in our truth and desperately try to hide what we perceive as inadequacy. We cloak ourselves with efforts to please, produce, and perform, hoping that our efforts will be enough. We cling to the covers of power or proficiency as we attempt to avoid being seen in our vulnerability. Envy rises around us, and we become convinced that if only we had what another has, we would be enough. We work hard at earning love, grasping for what we fear we don't deserve, ashamed of who we are because we have, for so long, believed that we don't measure up. Sadly, the noise of these messages can prevent us from hearing the voice of our heart that invites us to come home.

Shame escalates in the dark. As we hold it within and fail to give it a voice, it grows, sapping our energy and power. Shame, however, cannot survive in the light because truth melts the lies that sustain it. To release our shame, we must name it; we must peel back the layers and masks behind which we've hidden for so long. We simply ask for the grace to stand in the Presence of Unbounded Love, who peels away these old and sticky patterns.

Come Home

Slowly we learn that what we need to fill the empty place is actually inside our heart, within ourselves.

Naming and letting go of these layers can be painstakingly slow, demanding a discipline of honesty, courage, and patience to be faithful. This is not a place to rush but a process of walking step by step, not missing a beat, honoring the learning as each layer falls away. We often seek soul-companions along this walk, those who can stand with us, gently encouraging us and witnessing with compassion as we remove the masks. In that safe space, we can assume a position of honesty, allowing ourselves to see the truth.

In this process we are continually invited to come home to ourselves. As we become more attentive to the voice of our heart, the long-held lies fall aside, and we are able to stand in the truth and beauty of who we are. We strive less often to be someone else and stay faithful to our own voice. Once the shame has been washed away, we are able to hear our heart and trust our own way of knowing. Not unlike the prodigal son of Scripture (see Luke 15), we, too, come home to ourselves after wandering for so long. With the release of each layer, we are able to rest more securely where we belong—at home in our heart. Once these binding lies fall away, we are able to stand in truth and walk with new energy and freedom. In letting go of shame, we come home to the abundance that has been ours all along!

Suggested Reflection Process ♪

Darken a room, light a small candle, and sit quietly for several minutes. You may want to listen to some simple music (I recommend a cello CD, *The Poet*, by Michael Hoppe), and feel the soul tones within yourself. In the darkness, with your face turned away from the candlelight, name or feel the patterns of shame you carry with you. Then, gently and gradually, with your hand on your cheek, turn your face back to the light and invite yourself to come home to the truth, that you can be seen here and be loved. You may choose to use simple gestures of holding your shame and naming it in the light. Sit. Stay. Know that you are held here in Unbounded Love.

23. The Weavers

Walking in Community

*F*or the last twelve years, I have been blessed to gather with a sacred circle of women who explore the weaving of God in the fabric of their lives. Using ritual, reflection, and soul-sharing, this faith community has served as a source of grace and wisdom for many of us on our soul-journey. Always seated in a circle, we have become witnesses to our shared stories as, amid the struggles of life, we walk together in hope. The community woven from this experience has reached well beyond the parameters of the times and places of these gatherings, offering continued support and connections as we each, in turn, weave among the many others in our lives.

The Weaving Circle offers a safe communal container in which we can be seen and honored in our truth, renewed to return with focus and integrity to the tasks of each of our lives. It is a place of sharing the sacred soul-stories of our God experiences and the myriad ways we are called to mirror that Mystery.

These weavers model the essence and vital role of community in each of our lives as we are commissioned to walk together in faith. Using the image of a woven fabric, we know both the strength and the beauty that are created when numerous fibers and strands of various colors and textures are woven together. We know the warmth of being enfolded in a softly woven garment and the protection it offers in the cold. There is even the delight of the dance of the unwoven fringe that reminds us of the unfinished edges that hang free. All of these images speak of the elements and roles of a vital faith community in our lives.

The Weavers

We were not made to walk in isolation but, in fact, long for companions who can share with us this journey of the soul. We find or create a community of companions who will join us as we explore and expand our experience of the Sacred. We each long for a container that will receive us in our truth and support us as we grapple with the mysteries of life and God. We see a circle that will support us as we reach out in service, knowing that our efforts are amplified when joined with other hearts and hands. When these communities are energizing, compassionate, and inclusive, they reflect the expansive heart of the holy One who holds us all.

We have experienced the power of community when we have shared resources and gifts in various groups, some perhaps quite structured, others loosely woven. As we seek a faith community, we long for others who will embrace the deep soul-space within, joining us on the spiritual path. We gather together in our churches, synagogues, masques, and homes so that we might explore and implore the Mystery we so long to mirror. We hunger for a communal expression of joy and celebration, pain and loss, believing and knowing, that gathered together we are given the gifts of strength, courage, and compassion to live and act in love.

There are times, of course, when we find ourselves on the fringes of these communities, either hanging on the edge or perhaps expanding the weaving into something larger and new. Maybe we are presently in search of a faith community that will meet us with more authenticity on this journey. The good news is that community continues to be woven in and with our lives as we search for ways of connecting at the level of the Sacred. It is a hopeful venture as we walk forward together in faith, continuing to weave the unconditional love of the Holy in our lives and in our world.

Suggested Reflection Process 🌿

Sit with some of your experiences and stories of community. Using colors, words, or fibers, create an expression of the circles that have held you in the development of your faith. As you explore this theme, be sure to include not only the communities of formal religion but also the smaller faith communities that have been part of your history.

As you sit with the unwoven fringe in the painting, "The Weavers," use the above process to describe the faith communities you either long for in your life or vision in the future.

24. Risk the Sacred Journey

Facing the Future

*E*ach of us stands at the gate of tomorrow, facing the future. At times, we have walked in wonder and awe; at other times, we have moved along in the flood of fear. Looking back, we may recognize that amid the joys and the struggles of this journey, we have been companioned by a grace-full Presence that has held us together and led us on. This is not simply a journey through a string of days and years. Rather, this is a sacred journey, one that is held in and surrounded by Mystery. Although we long for someone to translate the risks of this journey into logical explanations, we often find ourselves in the foreign land of faith. We stand on the edge of our hopes and dreams and ask in trust to be led and supported by a Love and Energy much larger than we can imagine. We ask to walk here in courage and integrity, as we attempt to discern the voice of God amid the cacophony of our doubt and fear.

All the five-year plans in the world can't guarantee a predicted unfolding of the future. As much as we would like to pretend we are in control, we eventually recognize the illusion, and we sense that we stand naked before the unknown. This realization may awaken our deepest fears as we become overwhelmed with the risks of the journey ahead. Questions flood our mind and heart as we struggle with "How?" and "Why?" and "When?" and "Why me?" Our anxiety rises as we wonder if we will have what we need to meet the challenges before us. We consider changing our course, perhaps dismissing our dreams and retreating to the safe patterns of our past. In these moments, the comfortable status quo subtly calls us back, away from the risk of integrity. We doubt our discernment and second guess the song of our soul that has lured us to this edge of action. There, as the winds of change whip around us, we wonder What or Who really calls us into tomorrow.

But the future may also awaken an excitement, an energy full of hopes, visions, and dreams. Fortified with focused fires of determination and commitment, we boldly embrace the challenges of change. An adrenaline-like grace flows through us, and nothing can deter us from our goal. Dauntlessly we engage all of our energies, and those of the companions gathered with us, to effect transformation. Hope is high as we face the obstacles that rise in our path, knowing in faith that we will be led and companioned here.

As we stand on the edge of this sacred journey, the layers of memories and stories become our teachers. We wear a coat of many colors, woven of our days and nights of living and loving. The gifts of faith, trust, and courage intertwine with our doubts and fears as we stand between what we have known and what is yet to be. As our recollections of delight and clarity are layered with memories of barren doubt, confusion, and despair, we turn to the stories of faith that remind us of the gifts we have been given to be faithful. We remember the wisdom mirrored by our guides and mentors as we breathe into the center of our being where we are connected with the Wisdom of Sophia.

To risk the journey and face the future is simply to walk in faith, for there are no linear words that capture the massive Mystery of God. We stand as the figure in this painting, clothed in grace and showered with blessing. At times, we see the flecks of light; at other times, we see only the shadow of the silhouette. But always, both in our knowing and in our unknowing, we are escorted into tomorrow by Love, who gives us everything we need.

Suggested Reflection Process ࣶ

Spend a few minutes with the painting, "Risk the Sacred Journey." Where in the image are you drawn? As you face the future, what are the hopes and dreams that call you forward? What are your fears? What do you look like as you stand on the edge of tomorrow? What garment is woven of your memories of previous journeys? As you reflect on these questions, monitor what you feel in your body. What is your breathing like? Do you experience any tension or relaxation in your muscles?

Give this reflection voice by translating it into a dance. Remember that the movements can be as simple as standing and taking a step forward and then one or two steps backward. Use your arms and hands to express you feelings of courage, fear, etc.

When you finish, you may choose to reflect further on the theme by writing or drawing.

25. Roots of Light

Connecting with the Sacred

*T*his piece painted itself. After laying down a thick, dark strip of blue and green pigment, I squirted on globs of yellow and orange. I watched in amazement as the gold extended her arms into the green and the light began to root itself in the darkness. It was too cool! I immediately called a friend into the room to witness the simple and profound marriage of color that was happening right in front of me. This painting, finished in less than ten minutes, held the mystery of eternity and a map for our journey home to light.

When I sat with this piece, I was drawn to Jessica Power's poem, "The Ledge of Light," in which she writes:

> I have climbed up out of narrow darkness
> on to a ledge of light.
> I am of God; I was not made for night.

She later continues:

> God is a thousand acres to me now
> of high sweet-smelling April and the flow
> of windy light across a wide plateau.

Roots of Light

Ah, but when love grows unitive I know
joy will upsoar, my heart sing, far more free,
having come home to God's infinity.[3]

Sometimes, mired in the muck of our lives, we forget that we were created to be happy. We define ourselves by our pain and cling to our stance as victims of many wounds. We so want to be freed of these binds but, at the same time, we resist letting go, fearing no one will understand or believe us without them. We must remember that to own the light is not to deny the darkness but to allow it to be transformed—and it takes courage to be faithful to this transformative process. The pain must first be named in honesty, explored with integrity, and honored with love. We cannot do it alone. Our prayer is to simply ask for what we need to walk this path. We gradually, but eventually, move out of our narrow darkness into the expansiveness and immensity of the holy One.

As we walk this journey of the soul, we are more and more able to see with clarity the goodness in which we were created. God, so deeply rooted in our being, continues to transform our darkness into light, walking with us to that ledge of life where we finally recognize how deeply we are loved.

Like the process of this painting, we are called to stand in awe at the unfolding miracle of being loved and the surprise that greets us when we finally open our heart to receive. The fullness of the insight still awaits us, but insights are given when we recognize those roots of light and love in our life. The hope of our future is held in our heart and the hearts of our companions and our universe. As we face the future, walking between what is now and what is yet to be, may we take hope and courage from knowing that those roots of light connect us to the Source of all we will ever need. May we taste each day the sweetness of this loving God who calls us by name and reminds us, "You belong to me. I will give you all you need!"

Suggest Reflection Process ꝣ

We connect to this ledge of light when we recall that we are created in love. An ancient, four-line mantra of the Eastern tradition carries that reminder. It is a prayer for ourselves asking that we might be filled with the light we so long for.

Go for a walk, and slowly and mindfully repeat the following phrases. Allow the words to steep inside, praying that you might be open to these gifts.

May I be filled with loving-kindness.
May I be well.
May I be peaceful and at ease.
May I be happy.

Use this mantra over an extended period of time until the words become rooted in your mind and heart. Once you have grounded yourself in loving kindness, begin sending this prayer to others as you ask that they, too, be filled with loving kindness, are well, peaceful, at ease, and happy. Let the rhythm of the repetition root you in the light, as each day you face the future on this journey of your soul.

Notes

1. Abram J. Klausner. *The Bicentennial Passover Haggadah* (Yonkers, NY: Emanual Press Publication, 1976).

2. *Julian of Norwich* Showings, translated from the critical text with an introduction by Edmund Colledge, O.S.A. and James Walsh (Mahwah, NJ: Paulist Press, 1978).

3. *Selected Poetry of Jessica* Powers, edited by Regina Siegfried, ASC, and Robert F. Morneau (Kansas City, MO: Sheed and Ward, 1989).